AWAKENING
∽ *your* ∽
SENSE
∽ *of* ∽
WONDER

Other books by the author:

The Heart of a Runaway
Managing Your Restless Search
If My Kids Drive Me Crazy, Am I A Bad Mom?
When Your Marriage Disappoints You
Friends Forever
The Island Mansion Mystery

Other books coauthored with Stephen Bly:

Winners and Losers
Questions I'd Like to Ask
The Crystal Adventure Series
How To Be a Good Man
Be Your Mate's Best Friend
How To Be a Good Grandparent
Fox Island
Copper Hill

AWAKENING *your* SENSE *of* WONDER

Discovering God in the Ordinary

JANET CHESTER BLY

Discovery House Publishers is affiliated with Radio Bible Class, Grand Rapids, Michigan 49501.

Discovery House books are distributed to the trade by Thomas Nelson Publishers, Nashville, Tennessee 37214.

Scripture references marked NIV are from the *Holy Bible: New International Version*, copyright © 1973, 1978, 1984 International Bible Society. Used by permission of Zondervan Bible Publishers.

Library of Congress Cataloging-in-Publication Data

Bly, Janet.
    Awakening your sense of wonder: discovering God in the
ordinary / Janet Chester Bly.
       p. cm.
    Includes bibliographical references.
    ISBN 1-57293-018-7
    1. Mystery. 2. God—Knowableness. 3. Wonder. 4. Awe.
I. Title.
BT127.5.B58 1997
242—dc20   96-44860
                                               CIP

For correspondence and information about speaking engagements:

Janet Chester Bly
P. O. Box 157
Winchester, Idaho 83555

For Russell
    For Michael
        For Aaron

May the eyes of your hearts be enlightened

CONTENTS ⤳

One

LIKE MEN WHO DREAM
How we lost it and why

> *Wonder*
> *lies cold*
> *hard and yellowed*
> *like corn kernels tossed*
> *on a black cast-iron world.*

*T*he sun briefly burned off the foggy haze and pushed through the clouds. The snows drained into splashing puddles and trickling creeks. Not a day for sensible people to be sloshing outside, muddying their shoes.

And on my to-do list: six shirts and three blouses to iron, a half dozen get-well cards to send, an outline for this book to type, a new crop of cobwebs to dust, and delightful menus to plan from a half-empty cupboard. But Miranda wanted to hike to the bridge.

So we set out for the state park just down the road, stopping to read signs, guessing who or what had made the prints in the drifts, and picking up treasures and litter, egg-shaped stones and pop cans. When we reached the bridge, I stood for a moment with the four-year-old, then turned to go back home.

"But, Grandma," a small voice said, "look at all the trails on the other side. I've never been on all of those."

Miranda was the leader as she plowed down narrow, winding paths, over boulders, and around fallen timbers. Then, she suddenly stopped. "Look, an F-stick!"

She picked up a small limb with two horizontal bends. A few steps later she reached for another stick, insisting it was an I. "Grandma," she exclaimed, "this forest has letters in it. Let's find all the words and make a story!"

Most children have a measure of it: the ability to see the wonder, the stories in the forest. We have a taste of it when we've first embraced a brand-new experience or found an intriguing place or begun a relationship where everything's fresh and full of adventure and delightful discoveries, such as when we enter into friendship with God through Christ.

But many lose their sense of wonder along the way. A pall of mundane and ordinary and routine sets in. It's like the constant fight against dust and dirt and clutter in our houses. If we don't attack it on a daily basis, we're inundated with thingies on the floor and clouds on the furniture and piles everywhere, and we can't simply relax and enjoy home. The same is true with our sense of wonder. It becomes dulled or stunted, even deadened, under the stifling clutter poured into everyday living.

Sometimes a child's delightful commentary or a poignant event or a sovereign supernatural intervention jump-starts our dead spirits and revives our sight again, so we fully appreciate and enjoy this temporary abode and see pieces of the enticing blueprints of the dwelling that is to come.

Miranda and I tried to find some of the stories in the forest that day. We sat very still and listened to the quiet end-of-winter sounds. We could hear a few birds singing, a squirrel running and chattering, a truck braking on a far-away road, and Miranda thought she could detect snoring from the sleeping trees that had fallen on the forest floor.

Perhaps some night we'll come here with a tent and listen to the night noises and sniff the camp aromas and hug the trees and feel the rough bark and sticky sap. Someday we'll go deeper, try to learn the stories beneath the surface: about why the mighty ponderosas grow here and how old they are; about what each plant and flower and wild rose is called, how they smell, and what creatures live in their shadows; about the loggers who once milled here, the Indians who hunted here; about the floods and storms and historic gatherings and famous persons who visited. And we'll still only scratch that surface. Wonder can grow on any spot on this earth.

Wonder: What It Is

Wonder is *something we see or perceive that causes our spirits to soar and our minds to marvel at a world we discover beyond our own.*

The sense of wonder is:
- seeing things in a fresh new way—the old and familiar jump out with new meanings and give hints that maybe there's more.
- looking at life backward. What we seem to lose is really gain. What looks like a downer means we're on the

way up. Real life is a paradox. Victory comes through
defeat, healing through brokenness, finding ourselves
through giving ourselves away.[1]

- the masterpiece quality of the human soul, something
  we have in common with angels. No other creature
  down here has it. It happens when our minds are
  overwhelmed by something totally beyond our
  imagination or expectation.
- deliverance when all hope is gone. Psalm 126 vividly
  pictures people filled with wonder when God brought
  them back home after long years of captivity.

> . . . we were like men who dreamed. Our mouths were
> filled with laughter, our tongues with songs of joy. Then
> it was said among the nations, "The LORD has done
> great things for them." The LORD has done great things
> for us, and we are filled with joy (Psalm 126:1–3).

Wonder is the ability to be amazed or offer sincere
respect or count some things as sacred. We grow in
wonder when we recognize higher authorities, more
superior abilities, and when we allow the attitude of awe
and appreciation to rule, rather than skepticism and
resentment.

Wonder is a moment of enlightenment, a "graced
moment," when the humdrum tingles with excitement,
when we're faced with a scene straight out of heaven's
drama or tranquility.

Wonder is a long-range view into tomorrow. Wonder is the sum of "countless joys that ever flow" from God.[2] Wonder is seeing with the heart and soul and spirit.

We read and hear about many wonders, but when we actually witness them, their grandeur or power often surpasses our comprehension: flying low over the crater of Mount Saint Helens, hunkering down in the fury of Hurricane Ella, standing alone in the presence of the angel Gabriel. Or seeing your newborn for the very first time.

Some wonders aren't recognized until they're taken from us. "Sleep, riches, and health," the sign said on the donut-shop wall, "are not appreciated until they are interrupted."

Wonder includes elements of complete surprise, the totally unexpected, or the utter amazement that something you longed for actually materializes and is as satisfying or even more incredible than you imagined. Those on the verge of wonder can be riddled with doubts, but they can't quite stifle their curiosity.

We try to experience wonder on our own. We seek it in the multimillion-dollar fairyland of Disney World or in a science-fiction thriller or in a drug high. We hope for it in an exotic vacation trip or in a new love or in the teasing possibility that we might win a fabulous lottery. We pray for it during times of danger, in the healing of diseases, and in the reconciling of bitter relationships.

Elisha witnessed it in the middle of a war zone— surrounded by an invisible army of horses and chariots of fire. James, John, and Peter spied wonder on a mountain-top: Jesus shining as a glorious being. Stephen felt it while being stoned—the canvas of heaven ripped open before him.[3]

Corrie ten Boom felt it in the gracious whispers of mercy amid the horrors of a concentration camp: in the form of God-appointed fleas, in the timely appearance of a sweetly singing bird flying a loop above her head, and in the dream vision from her dead sister, telling Corrie to minister to the world.[4]

I sensed it one day in 1967. I was hanging clothes on the line in the backyard of our small farmhouse. Storm clouds began to fill the sky and as they scudded by, one of those wonder holes sprayed through, a gush of circular sun rays like a hearty halo on the fields. The display coincided with a long season of spiritual seeking, and it left me with a strange longing.

A natural phenomenon like this is common and can be easily explained by probing the structure of the sky and the elements of the atmosphere. But for many—even those with the understanding of the scientific mechanics and data, those with the sense of wonder—these experiences cause us to consider the spiritual realm, to wonder at these celestial signs and hints in the heavens.

The scene that day jarred me to ask aloud for the first time: "Is there a God? Is He real? If so, what is He like? And would He care to befriend a person like me?"

Above our heads every day unfolds an incredible spectacle, a ceaseless pageant—sometimes menacing, sometimes a swirling canvas of artistic elegance, a sometimes eerie, sometimes gentle and soothing kind of breathtaking magic. And the force of sunlight forging through the various mix of gases and particles in the air produces fiery fantasias and global light shows. "I always think of the second coming of Christ," I've often heard people say. The nineteenth-century British author John Ruskin described this kind of aerial theatrics as "almost human in its passions, almost spiritual in its tenderness, almost divine in its infinity."[5]

When wonder appears, it may have the smell and feel of something "old, ancient, having existed before the beginning of time." It also has an air of eternity about it, a foretaste of heaven.[6]

Joy can be a part of wonder's essence, but not its fullness. Joy is a new pair of bright white Reeboks to replace the grungy year-old pair. Wonder is a well-fitting pair of shoes, suddenly appearing for a homeless child the day before school starts. Joy is the welcome-home greeting when you return home after an absence. Wonder is feeling God's forgiving smile. Joy is recognizing a song from your school days on the radio. Wonder is losing yourself in a concert of symphonies and concertos and billowing overtures. Joy is making peace with an enemy. Wonder contemplates all God is and revels in the knowledge that He's still on our side.

Wonder is more than novelty stirring the sensual pleasure nodes. It's such a rounding and stretching and expanding of the soul that it influences the entire personality. It has staying power and changing power. It "touches the heart, addresses the will, molds the mind."[7] A sacred sighting may last only a moment, but its wondrous impact lingers pleasantly in your memory.

It's eyeing "gilded scenes of shining prospects . . . while treading on classic ground."[8] It's the first time or best time we view an amazing sight, something that makes the eyes dance and the heart sing.

A friend returned to college at age forty-five and reported after a few weeks, "I will never see the world around me in the same way. I've always felt that the earth I stand on is solid and motionless and that the sky above me is a flat sheet with a few stars sprinkled across it. Today I watched a video of the constant, violent motion under the oceans and in the hearts of mountains and in the air around us. Then, we studied from an observatory the multitudes of star clusters, nebulae, galaxies, and the meteors and comets that slash through them all. I still haven't gotten my balance back. It's as if I need to regain my land legs."

She's developing her sense of wonder.

What Wonder Does for Us

Wonder expands our thinking, deepens our insight, attunes our hearing. We begin to ask, Why? and How? and What if? Out of that quest comes discovery: all of our inventions and creations and musings and pushing for knowledge—our drive to conquer challenges, to search out mysteries. It should lead somewhere, prod us to think a bigger thought that moves on to nobler or more expansive actions. Visions and insights that open us to wonder should be enjoyed and meditated on and pondered through the years until we not only understand their meaning, but find ourselves shaped by them.[9]

A sense of wonder exposes the world as more than flat and static and still. We become able to see its dynamic qualities, to see inside and through and past the obvious. Wonder recognizes and enjoys the beauty of creation and the quality of created things.

When we develop the sense of wonder we gain insight into purposes and meanings behind events and gain the desire to seek out wisdom from the powers beyond our own. We're able to understand that this life isn't all there is. There's a time and space and order in another dimension.

Wonder helps us perceive the winsomeness in another human being, to feel more than just pity, to want to participate in that person's pain.

Wonder overpowers us, catches us up in something grand and marvelous outside ourselves. So much of life is full of moments that seem so real as we experience them, but they quickly pass and fade into memory. We can't possess them or keep them. We can't get into them and stay. This in itself is a hint that our world isn't concrete, solid, permanent. It's a mirage that glistens like sharp glass in the sun one moment but is shattered and gone the next. The human heart is restless and raging, trying this and dabbling in that, hoping to find fulfillment, to possess something that will give us innocence, identity. Our hearts want something glorious that lasts.[10]

Wonder keeps us moving to accomplish goals with a sense of purpose, heightens our motivations, keeps us fighting the winds of adversity rather than drifting in a senseless sea. We're driven to make the most of opportunities to bring a touch of eternity to another's heart. Each circumstance is an opportunity for spiritual good, each place a chance to do a holy deed. A sense of wonder provides keen spiritual perspective that's best balanced with earthy common sense.

A sense of wonder pulls us out of ourselves and into a worthier object—something bigger, someone finer, somewhere far greener.

Wonder nourishes and refreshes the spirit and releases the springs of divine joy. It encourages the disheartened, the hopeless, and the helpless. "Yes, there is a God," we exclaim, "and perhaps He cares for me."

Wonder helps us grasp the concept of eternity, investigate the world's spiritual counterpart, consider God's existence.

A sense of wonder is the basis for worship and praise of God. We're alert to catching Him at His work, watching for the love and mercy and justice He pours onto our planet every day. Without a sense of wonder, we sleep through all the good parts.

Wonder has an attitude of thankfulness, reverence, giving the attention back to God. It is assuming "that God is alive, and that wonderful news from Him is likely to break through at any moment."[11]

Wonder Is Not for Everyone

The world will never starve for wonders; but only for want of wonder.[12]

To talk of the need for a sense of wonder to some folks sounds like nonsense, delving into the ethereal, the otherworldly—in other words, stuff that's totally irrelevant. To them the whole subject smacks of sentimentality, superficiality, an unwillingness to face the hard facts of real life. "What you see is what you get," they taunt. Wonder is for kids who are ignorant or naive, who are easily impressed because they don't know any better, don't know how things work, haven't yet conquered any vistas that give them the sense of being masters of their fate.

However, at some point we become saturated with the secular, the earthy sensual, the material, the compulsion—born of the fear that this is all there is—to reap all we can from this day. We become overwhelmed with our needs, our problems, our adversities, our turmoils, our weaknesses. We're overcome by sorrows and uncertainties and burdens. We're overrun by despair and misery, emptiness and shame, dangers and fears, confusion and chaos. We want more, but who has the energy and time to assimilate wonder?

Arrogance crucifies wonder. Deceit and suspicion make it difficult to discern. Poor nurturing in childhood stunts it. A heart that's closed to people cools it. A callous conscience becomes a "drunkenness of soul."13

The wonderless quickly forget a kindness done or any benefits awarded them.

The wonderless are indifferent, stoic. We recognize them by their fat hearts, dull ears, sluggish eyes. They have large, empty spaces between their thoughts and connections to a purpose larger than themselves. They fight to get and keep control. They stand rigidly stationed at the hub of their universe. Nothing's sacred except what affects them personally.

Those with a sense of wonder irritate the wonderless—their comforts are disturbed. Wonder's fervency feels like a foreign intrusion; it gets labeled "misguided," "immature," "irrational."

Wonder reminds the wonderless of the unknown, those things out of their control or outside of their experience: mysteries to be solved, meanings to unravel, spiritual realities to face.

A sense of wonder can be a bother. It takes time and energy to see deeply. Wondering disrupts and muddles peace and tranquility. Wonder stirs fires. Wonder opens strange doors. Wonder finds stories in the forest when it's so much easier to plow through and get on home.

The wonderless ignore the signs and sights and sounds beneath the surface. Their zest is for trifles. Their major is minors. They're not interested in the wonder of it all. It's too much for the emaciated, starving soul to absorb.

John Alexander writes in *The Other Side* magazine, "A few years ago, I went to a free outdoor concert. It wasn't any old concert. Van Cliburn was playing a Tchaikovsky concerto with the Philadelphia Orchestra—Eugene Ormandy conducting. That kind of wonderful sound you get to hear live only a few times in one lifetime. In front of me sat half a dozen teenagers. Eating popcorn. . . . They might as well have been listening to a player piano."[14]

That scene became a metaphor of the way many of us live in God's universe. With little wonder. Little respect.

We become "a pair of spectacles behind which there is no eye."15

Elizabeth Barrett Browning said it this way:

> *Earth's crammed with heaven,*
> *And every common bush afire with God:*
> *But only he who sees, takes off his shoes;*
> *The rest sit round it, and pluck blackberries.*

Trauma or tragedy or injustice that embitters the soul also shrivels wonder. A critical, suspicious mind dims the light of wonder. It's like loathing fresh air and wanting to close all windows forever.

> Well, there are minds like that, that hate fresh air, that love a stuffy, overbreathed atmosphere, that are terrified of draughts even when it is the winds of God that are blowing through the earth.16

In C. S. Lewis's novel, *The Last Battle,* most of the main characters arrive on a sunlit summer morning at the framework of a doorway—nothing else, no walls, no roof—a door that seemed to lead from nowhere to nowhere. When the door opened, they saw darkness through the doorway as if it were night, though all around them was a glorious world of bright wonders. Some dwarfs huddled nearby in a circle, seeing only the blackness, feeling only the darkness, and smelling only the dung odors of a stable. Several of the characters urge them to look around and see the sky and the trees and the flowers. But the dwarfs only see themselves shut up in a dark hole.

"Oh, the poor things! This is dreadful," said Lucy. Then she had an idea. She stooped and picked some wild violets. "Listen, Dwarf," she said. "Even if your eyes are wrong, perhaps your nose is all right: can you smell that?" She leaned across and held the fresh, damp flowers to Diggle's ugly nose. But she had to jump back quickly in order to avoid a blow from his hard little fist.

"None of that!" he shouted. "How dare you! What do you mean by shoving a lot of filthy stable-litter in my face? There was a thistle in it too.

You're still at your old game. Starting a new lie! Trying to make us believe we're none of us shut up, and it ain't dark, and heaven knows what."[17]

Later in the story, Aslan, the lion, explains their dilemma.

"You see," said Aslan. "They will not let us help them. They have chosen cunning instead of belief. Their prison is only in their own minds, yet they are in that prison; and so afraid of being taken in that they can not be taken out."[18]

The wonderless pride themselves on their intelligence, on their control, on their ability to assess fact from fiction, realism from fantasy. They're "so afraid of being taken in that they can not be taken out"—taken out of their ruts, out of their apathy, out of themselves.

But even those with a highly developed sense of wonder can be wonderless when it comes to a particular subject.

For instance, some see old cars as rattletraps. Others view them as works in progress. "One man's trash is another man's treasure" can apply to the world of wonder where one's insight and interpretation can be very selective.

Can Wonder Be Developed?

> Jesus asked, "Do you see anything?"
> He looked up and said, "I see people; they look like trees walking around."
> Once more Jesus put his hands on the man's eyes. Then his eyes were opened, his sight was restored, and he saw everything clearly (Mark 8:23–25).

Is wonder developed by growing in knowledge—reading every *National Geographic* we can get our hands on? Or watching lots of *Moody* science films? Traveling to distant lands? Meditating in the quiet places of our spirits?

Is it dependent upon careful nurturing in our formative early years? Or do we have to wait for a sovereign event from heaven that makes us tremble with terror or glory? Do we only need our eyes opened, our sight restored, so we see everything around us more clearly? Or is it an ability we're born with, or not, and that's that?

Exploring the Wonder

1. What book, movie, experience, or person has most opened your mind or emotions to the sense of wonder?

2. Rank these scenarios in numerical order according to the degree of "wonder" they would be to you. Explain your top three choices.

___ schizophrenia completely healed through counseling
___ a cure for AIDS
___ a cure for cancer
___ a cure for the common cold
___ no more taxes
___ someone lives to be 150 years old
___ the second coming of Jesus Christ
___ life discovered on another planet
___ a couple happily married fifty years
___ permanent peace in the Middle East
___ complete elimination of the national debt
___ a whole year of no murders
___ your most fervent prayer request granted
___ racial prejudice eradicated
___ no more headaches
___ a loved one raised from death
___ a broken relationship restored
___ an unlimited line of credit
___ a date with a movie star
___ becoming a concert pianist
___ no more illicit sex, violence, or profanity in movies
___ other:

3. Which of the following amazes you? frightens you? excites you? angers you? bores you? Why?

- technological advances
- scientific discoveries
- spiritual revelations
- mechanical operations
- prophetic predictions
- supernatural miracles
- medical research
- religious conversions
- psychological insights
- social revolutions
- human transformations
- computer upgrades
- psychic phenomenon
- genetic engineering
- political debates
- astrology signs

4. Where do you think you're most likely to see or sense a thing of wonder? Explain.

❏ in a private chapel
❏ in a crowded sanctuary
❏ when walking with friends
❏ while alone on a mountaintop
❏ in a prison cell
❏ while gazing out your kitchen window
❏ while deathly sick in a hospital
❏ at a revival meeting
❏ during a prayer vigil
❏ other:

5. Read Psalm 126.
   Have you ever experienced times like this?
   What lesson did you learn?

6. Read 1 Chronicles 15.

What part of this scene could stir the sense of wonder?

Why do you think David's wife Michal felt like she did (verse 29)?

What prevented her from "entering in"?

7. Read Mark 8:23–26.

Why do you think Jesus had to touch the man's eyes a second time?

Notes

1. Charles Colson, *Loving God,* quoted in Reflections, *Christianity Today,* 14 May 1990, 33.
2. John Kendrick Bangs, quoted in Ralph L. Woods, ed. & comp., *A Treasury of Contentment* (New York: Simon & Schuster, Trident Press, 1969).
3. 2 Kings 6:15–17; Matthew 17:1–8; Acts 7:54–56.
4. Corrie ten Boom with John Sherrill and Elizabeth Sherrill, *The Hiding Place* (Carmel, N. Y.: Guideposts Associates, 1971).
5. John Ruskin, quoted in Oliver E. Allen, et. al. *Planet Earth—Atmosphere* (Alexandria, Va.: Time-Life Books, 1983), 6.

6. Peter J. Kreeft, *Heaven, the Heart's Deepest Longing* (San Francisco: Harper & Row, 1980).

7. Richard J. Foster and James Bryan Smith, eds., *Devotional Classics* (San Francisco: HarperCollins, HarperSan Francisco, 1993), 1.

8. Joseph Addison, quoted in *John Bartlett's Familiar Quotations* (Boston: Little, Brown, 1980), 325.6.

9. Foster and Smith, *Devotional Classics,* 2.

10. Joni Eareckson Tada, *Heaven, Your Real Home* (Grand Rapids: Zondervan, 1995), 117.

11. Arthur J. Gossip, "The Clash of Age and Youth," *Twenty Centuries of Great Preaching,* vol. 8 (Waco: Word, 1971), 245.

12. G. K. Chesterton, quoted in *John Bartlett's Familiar Quotations,* 742.8.

13. John Wesley, *The John Wesley Reader,* comp. Al Bryant (Waco: Word, 1983).

14. John Alexander, *The Other Side,* January-February 1989, quoted in Reflections, *Christianity Today,* 17 March 1989, 33.

15. Thomas Carlyle, quoted in *The New Dictionary of Thoughts* (New York: Standard Book Co., 1955), 713.

16. Gossip, "Clash of Age and Youth," 245.

17. C. S. Lewis, *The Last Battle,* vol. 7 in *The Chronicles of Narnia* (New York: Religious Book Club, 1973), 137.

18. Ibid., 139–40.

∽ *Two* ∽

A WORLD OF HIDE-AND-SEEK
Developing the sense of wonder

*I see and hear the signs of his return
That vagabond, the Sun, that nightly rover;
His brilliant fingers grasp the top of yonder hill,
And, very soon, he will be climbing over.*

Helen Nelson

*H*ow do we come to see the sun as a "vagabond," or a "nightly rover"? Or at what point do we marvel that the sun comes up at all? Do only poets have the eyes of wonder?

What does it take to open the spirit, to hone the senses? What does it take to reveal how blind we are? Sometimes we're the last to know, until the light is switched on. Once we know, does enlightenment come from our seeking or from God's initiation?

To Begin: A Spark
We need the spark of an inward or outward nudge to see the world in its true state of wonder.

Actress Dixie Carter tells about her grandmother who had a spontaneous way of trying to stir wonder in her grandchildren. She'd shout at them with great urgency: "Halbert Leroy Carter Jr.! Dixie Virginia Carter! Melba Helen Carter!"

When they ran to answer her summons, she'd say, "Stop! Look at God's beautiful sunset!"[1]

We're blind without teachers—seeing-eye guides—to force our attention up and out and beyond.

Helen Keller was, perhaps, the most famous deaf and blind person in the world. Her mind, as a child, was locked up in a prison cell due to an illness that struck before she was two years old. No sound, no light could get in. Her whole world consisted of what she could learn through touching. She was a wild thing, lacking any kind of control or social manners. Living in darkness and misunderstanding can make a person cranky! Helen needed discipline to unearth the mine of intelligence and sensitivity buried inside, to open the world of wonder.

"The most important day I remember in all my life," she wrote many years later, "is one on which my teacher, Anne Mansfield Sullivan, came to me. . . . On the afternoon of that eventful day, I stood on the porch, dumb, expectant. . . . I did not know what the future held of marvel or surprise for me."[2]

We all have blind spots. We're all deaf to some voices. We all experience the inability to communicate clearly, especially the depths of the longings and questions inside us, as well as the mysteries we find "out there." Someone must break through our ignorance and teach us the language, lead us by the hand, help us see with other eyes. We never know when a catalyst, such as an event or a person or a book or some new thought, will thrust us into the dawning of spiritual wonder in our lives.

When commanded to go to Rages, young Tobias

answered, "I do not know the way," and his father replied, "Go then and find someone to lead you."

Francis de Sales, a prolific writer in the late 1500s, described the mysteries of the spiritual world by using examples from the known physical world—simple, every-day images like bees and milk, birds and sugar. He had practical advice to give his friend Philothea: "You must most insistently beseech God to provide you with (a spiritual teacher) after his own heart. Have no misgivings in this regard for he who sent down an angel from heaven, as he did to young Tobias, will give you a good and faithful guide."[3]

A "restlessness and a spirit that cannot be consoled by the inner comforts that once brought them peace" often becomes the road to wonder.[4] But it may begin as simply as someone showing you the intricate beauties in one flower. Miniature rose hybridizer Ralph S. Moore says it this way:

> *Take my hand, walk with me,*
> *See what's in bloom today,*
> *Stroll down my garden path,*
> *We'll visit on our way.*

We Learn To See

In our attempts to understand what life is all about, we learn to see the world in its true state of wonder.

We must somehow take a wider view, look at the whole landscape, really see it, and describe what's going on here. Then we can at least wail the right question into the swaddling band of darkness, or, if it comes to that, choir the proper praise.[5]

Find out how things work, the reason behind every rule. Stimulate the mind by exchanging ideas, sharing doubts. Develop overviews, discover higher meanings, highlight clues to the secrets of the unknown. Even a slight turning, a gradually changing perspective, can put us well on the pathway of wonder.

Curiosity and reflection, listening to silence and venturing out, patiently watching and asking the ancient questions, spontaneous immersion by taking a first step, then another; we find when we seek. As our field of inquiry broadens, we're eager for more information. Developing the sense of wonder is an ongoing, lifetime process. As our spiritual lenses become more focused, as well as all encompassing, we can recognize a glimpse of wonder when we see it.

Knowing a name, a piece of information, charges any discovery with personal investment, any ordinary exchange with significance: the treasure leaps out. We discover by embracing a willingness to think, disciplining our minds to consider and assess our thoughts, and then humbly listening to what others have to say. We actively read or actively listen—even better, we do both.

Take music, for instance. We can know that a symphony or a concerto is supposed to be great music. That is, we're supposed to like and appreciate it and get all kinds of swelling inspiration from it. But we don't always, until someone helps us understand. We learn a bit of history that ties the piece in. We hear a story about the writer or about the philosophy behind the writing or about the event that triggered it. Or we see a movie (or cartoon!) that uses the piece as a theme. Or someone teaches us how to pick out for ourselves the melody and harmony, the repeating patterns, the rhythms, the comparison to other works, the form and theme. Active listening is a learned art. Music is a language in which we can gain a basic fluency. Appreciation comes through experience and knowledge, through hearing more deeply.

It's like watching people look through a microscope. Some glance for a moment, then shrug and move away. They see nothing. Others look for several moments and say, "How amazing," or "How beautiful." They see more, but not much more. Then there are those who look long and intently. They try to really see. They see shapes and patterns, likeness and difference, depth and change. The more we know of the object we are looking at, the more we see *in* it.[6]

We Sharpen Our Focus

When we sharpen our focus and enlarge our sensitivities, we learn to see the world in its true state of wonder.

Every day, those who are able walk somewhere: around the block, over to the elevator, out of the parking lot, or into the kitchen. Do we tend to look down, seeing only the next step in front of us, or to look up and around and ahead? Of course, there's always the fear of tripping over some obstacle. And we will, at times. But there's also the chance of missing some wondrous sight.

A few weeks ago I happened to look out the window of my back door just as a big, fat raccoon scampered up a neighbor's tree. There it was in all its glory—rings on its tail and a mask over its eyes. In all the years we've lived in Winchester, Idaho, I've never seen a raccoon. Nor have my neighbors, who've lived here much longer. This critter has been hidden from view. How many more surprises are hiding all around us, teasing us, daring us to spot them as they play hide-and-seek? We won't know unless we stay watchful in one place long enough—to see comparisons, changes, movements, and things coming out of hiding.

We can keep our eyes and hearts open to the heavens; we can try to peek through some mysterious closed door of knowledge. However, the mind, the brain—not the eyes—is our greatest instrument of discovery and understanding.

We can pick through the cluttered voices of our day, sorting out the important ones and tuning in.

We can take a step back from our world to see it more completely, to appreciate it more richly, to experience it more fully.

We can pause a moment and take a minivacation for the soul—a five-minute meditation, a weekend retreat, or a full-blown sabbatical.

We all need some measure of faithful instruction and nurture before we can reap a satisfying harvest in any endeavor, and that includes a harvest of wonder. But it definitely takes more than dry textbooks, dull lectures, or endless worksheets. We've also got to be looking for surprises. We've got to become active observers and develop the habit of responding compassionately to others.

To the measure that our minds lack the sense of wonder and sensitivity to worlds beyond our own, to that measure our hearts are capable of being filled with all kinds of malice—anger, bitterness, frustration—because we don't see, we don't understand what rages out there beyond our own rage. It's all noise and nuisance and harassment to us. We try to drown it out, instead, with too much activity— every waking moment planned, a constant barrage of electric entertainment. "The best and most beautiful things in the world cannot be seen," said Helen Keller. "They must be felt with the heart."

We Appreciate Small Pleasures

Our sense of wonder expands when we learn to appreciate the small, everyday pleasures.

"To me," said Walt Whitman, "every hour of the light and dark is a miracle, every cubic inch of space is a miracle."[7]

That's the way a growing baby sees the world. That's the way the once-I-was-blind-but now-I-can-see view the world.

Going through a door and being welcomed in. Getting in and becoming a part.

Digging deep into moist, rich soil.

Biting into a ripe, juicy nectarine. Sniffing freshly baked bread or popcorn or pizza. The senses of taste and smell "must still be rated as the chemical masterpieces of [the] body."[8]

Blue sky. Blue seas. A long, cool drink. Bread and butter.

The computer working. A parking space near the entrance. Waiting only five minutes at the doctor's office.

Pine needles. Wild grapes. Tulip trees. Little downy chicks. Pansies in pots. A miniature rose tree, eighteen inches high, plum-colored buds opening to tight double-lavender blooms. A lawn bursting with dandelions, splattered with dew and buzzing with bees. A single bird-of-paradise flower.

Jet streams like chalk marks scraping the horizon. A single scraggly bush on the empty lot. A child helping her little brother across the street.

To experience beauty, to receive a kindness, to discover a new friend.

Stillness.

A moment to rest.

To appreciate the little things is very practical. It makes us more peaceable, more ready to love, more pleasant to be around. It also alerts our senses to recognize the opening of the door to wonder.

We Recognize the Spiritual

The difference between the physical and the spiritual.

Whenever possible, get out of artificial environments. Get as close to the real, natural, earthy world as you can. Get away from the illusions of life and get into the wet, cold streams.

"A catching God's eye," Annie Dillard calls it.[9]

Fixing "our minds and our souls on the difference

between eternal realities and earthly realities," comments Teresa of Avila.[10]

> God has not hidden it or made it hard, but the eyes of many are too dim to the spiritual world.[11]

We may not see the spiritual until we detect the contrast, the comparisons with our familiar physical world. When studying the heavens with its multitude of shining spheres, distinguishing one from another depends upon knowing their relative sizes and magnitudes. Because all stars have nearly the same intrinsic brightness in infrared, their distances can be computed by comparing that intrinsic brightness with their observed brightness.[12]

We need some sense of the size of each star and planet— and a sense of the infinite regions of space in which they move—or there can be no true knowledge of the cosmos and its relation to this earth.[13]

Some wonders can be recognized only by comparing them to something else—for instance, the absolute glory of light after a long night of darkness.

The spiritual world is at least as vast as the physical world. And we have a difficult time attaining more than a superficial knowledge of our physical world through our five senses. We have to resort to other aids to see farther or deeper.

The Hubble space telescope, launched in 1990, serves as a pair of eyes viewing the wonders of deep, deep space and time. As it explores each corner of the universe it sends back pictures of galaxies at various stages of development.

It's an attempt to solve cosmological questions, to convey the awe-invoking beauty of the universe, and to peer back to the beginning of creation.[14]

But what can we use to see bits and pieces of the spiritual? It takes much more than a wide-field telescope, with or without color filter wheels.

God uses wonders of the physical world to alert us to spiritual wonders.

"He reveals deep and hidden things; he knows what lies in darkness, and light dwells with him. . . . There is a God in heaven who reveals mysteries" (Daniel 2:22, 28).

Now we're at a standstill. If we've followed all the previous suggestions, we're primed and ready, but we've got no other place to go. We've hit a stone wall. We can't go any further by ourselves.

Only God can open the barrier, the dividing wall, between this world and the next. At this point, all we can do is to watch, pray, and wait. We're at a point where we must have "the ability to see with the eyes of the soul—which God himself must open up to us. . . . Until God speaks—'Let there be light!'—a thick darkness covers the abyss of every soul."[15]

"Be still, and know that I am God" (Psalm 46:10).

"I call as my heart grows faint; lead me to the rock that is higher than I" (Psalm 61:2).

At some point we are startled to realize that it has not been all our doing. We have not initiated this adventure. It has not been entirely our idea. God Himself nudged us in the first place and He will complete the process. All we have to do is cooperate—want it to happen—and He will gladly open the door into the great and glorious other world. But in His time, His way.

Not only does something come if you wait, but it pours over you like a waterfall, like a tidal wave. You wait in all naturalness, without expectation or hope, emptied, translucent, and that which comes rocks and topples you; it will shear, loose, launch, winnow, grind.[16]

The ultimate goal of developing our sense of wonder is finding and experiencing a spiritual being—our heavenly Father.

Helen Keller tried to explain what it's like to be deaf and blind: "Have you ever been at sea in a dense fog, when it seemed as if a tangible white darkness shut you in, and the great ship, tense and anxious, groped her way toward the shore with plummet and sounding-line, and you waited with beating heart for something to happen? I was like that ship before my education began, only I was without compass or sounding-line, and had no way of knowing how near the harbor was. 'Light! give me light!' was the wordless cry of my soul, and the light of love shone on me in that very hour."[17]

The sleeping spirit can be awakened. The dead and dull and dwindling senses can come alive. The eyes of the blind can be opened. The signs that this has happened, or is about to happen, are many.

The spiritually stimulated may respond by singing praises, dancing spontaneous jigs, or shouting psalms. Or they may become very quiet—meditating on life, their new-

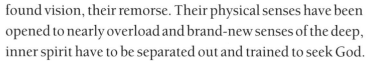

found vision, their remorse. Their physical senses have been opened to nearly overload and brand-new senses of the deep, inner spirit have to be separated out and trained to seek God.

What are some of the spiritual senses?

When we understand the fixed physical laws, we enter the explosion of scientific knowledge almost overnight. When we respect and abide by the laws of nature, we're launched into scientific enlightenment. Even so, spiritually we can still be in the Dark Ages. But learning about, respecting, and abiding by spiritual laws brings explosive personal change.

Over and above the sense of taste and touch and sight and smell and hearing stir deeper senses: a sense of the soft and pure, a sense of something freshly minted, senses like faith and hope and the confidence that anything is possible, a sense of amazement, of astonishment, of being overwhelmed, a sense of passionate zeal and jubilation, senses of thanksgiving and gratitude and a desire to celebrate someone else's successes, a sense of timelessness, of poetry in motion, of being retaught the loveliness of things, a sense that some things, some moments are sacred, a reverence for creation and people and almighty God.

Some seem born with it, a "barefooted soul,"[18] experiencing the tingling touch of heightened aesthetic sensibilities, spiritual splendor in the green and glossy grasses. Others need a direct meteorite hit.

The newly awakened know they are humble beginners. That's the way we always should see ourselves, for we are on a lifetime journey of constant discovery. The enormity of all we don't yet know makes our little that we do know a partial insight, a light that shines just a few steps ahead.

We're leaving our childish perceptions to become more insightful, a bit wiser. We're walking away from the foolishness of ignorance and into the privilege of knowledge. We're making out of the earthy ordinary a highly crafted universal purpose and meaning. We're finding our spiritual side. But it will never be a smooth, easy path. And we will never completely, totally understand everything, yet.

But "once the soul is opened and we know how to see beyond our *selves,* you could say, God will keep walking by."[19]

The Prize: Wonder

Helen Keller explains how her teacher was drawing water when she "placed my hand under the spout. As the cool stream gushed over one hand she spelled into the other the word *water,* first slowly, then rapidly. I stood still, my whole attention fixed upon the motions of her fingers. Suddenly I felt a misty consciousness as of something forgotten—a thrill of returning thought; and somehow the mystery of language was revealed to me. I knew then that 'w-a-t-e-r' meant the wonderful cool something that was flowing over my hand. That living word awakened my soul, gave it light, hope, joy, set it free!"[20]

True wonder is breathtaking!

The great round world with its "burning mountains, buried cities, moving rivers of ice."[21] People who recover from severe illness or injury or are freed from debilitating addiction. Catastrophe avoided in the nick of time. Ancient ruins and precious stones or polonium radiohalos. Radiant peace. An act of justice and mercy. Deep mourning turned to dancing. A joyous prophecy fulfilled. A tangled puzzle solved. The glory of victory, the mystery of love. Feeling the rumble of thunder deep within the chest.[22]

A rocket launch. The image of a superhot white dwarf (star) in a death throe. A total solar eclipse. Our planet's shadow on the moon. Discovering a new planet. Watching a meteorite shower or a fireball or a satellite orbiting overhead. Army jets, stunt-flying in perfect formation. Majestic mirror images on a lake's surface. A crimson bloom on a barrel cactus. Watercolor days, charcoal nights. Sweet and strange things locked up in the heart. A tornado or severe forest fire leaving pockets of untouched materials and survivors. Light lacing the edges of clouds that hide the full moon. The eternal horizon, dazzling with a million colors and streaks of light that dart and dance and die, where the earth and heavens seem sewn together.

An enchanted moment.

Truth that vibrates.

A glimpse of God's shadow; His marks, His fingerprints, His thumbnail, "straight down the middle of awe."[23]

> The whole show has been on fire from the word go . . . the whole world sparks and flames.[24]

But that doesn't mean every spirit-awakened soul sees the same things or applies the same interpretations. Everyone's not drawn to the same pool of delights. That's why it's good there's so many of them. We each have our own wonder pilgrimage, yet we can, if we will, draw from one another's pools. And often, wonder is best seen by looking back on an event—wonder in retrospect—especially as we see the context of all the things that followed after.

True wonder remains important for years to come—a lasting memory with an eternal purpose.

We will forever look differently at our world and live differently in it. We will assess separately the past, present, and future. Life, as we've known it, has forever been altered.

In just fifty-seven minutes, the *Galileo* probe upset a lot of expectations about the planet Jupiter. According to tests, Jupiter's composition is more like our sun than scientists had anticipated. Its thin clouds contain no water. Lightning is relatively rare and generates no complex organic molecules. The atmosphere is both denser and windier than scientists had calculated. They also found unexpected radiation belts. This mission's findings promise to change many theories about Jupiter and its origin, leaving scientists feeling awkward. "There's always a sense of humility when the data comes in," sighed the chief of the project. "The results don't fit our models very well . . . the shoe pinches!"[25]

The world beyond, the earth below

Some people seem to have a highly developed sense of wonder without any particular effort on their part. Others must engage in a slow, often deliberate, process. In either case, the reward is a gradual advancement from slumbering spirit to becoming fully human, vitally alive. This wonder should lead to practical responses—a prompting to want to do works of love, to want to do good deeds out of an enlightened desire and gratitude, to want to make creations of worth, of eternal value.

We traverse the vast distance from marveling at letter-shaped branches in the forest to gasping at the enormous sweep of the history of God and humankind and the cosmic purpose—a world far and away beyond our own, yet we recognize we're swept up in it, through the eyes of wonder.

Exploring the Wonder

1. When I think of the spiritual world, it seems to me (mark all that apply):
❑ nonexistent
❑ impenetrable
❑ none of my business
❑ too much for my dull brain
❑ a primitive idea of ignorant savages
❑ a world of wonder
❑ a place where I'd like to spend forever

2. One thing that has kept me from more fully entering into potential experiences of wonder has been:
❑ fear
❑ controversy

❏ hassles and problems
❏ duties and responsibilities
❏ uncertainty
❏ lack of desire
❏ other:

3. What do you think are the influences in our day that dull our spiritual senses?

4. Give a simple or a scientific explanation of how a rainbow is produced. What is supposed to be a spiritual meaning and purpose behind the physical display of the rainbow (see Genesis 9:12–17)?

When have you discovered a spiritual meaning behind a natural phenomenon?

5. Teresa of Avila, a very spiritual woman born in 1515 in southern Spain, once wrote: "Learning to draw water up from the spiritual well is a hard labor, indeed—at least in the beginning. It is difficult, in the first place, to keep all of your senses recollected and focused upon total humility before God."[26]

What do you think she meant by this?

What other comment would you add to her statement?

6. "It is he [God] who knows where the best drinking places are. In fact very often he is the one who with much effort and industry has provided the watering places."[27]

Rewrite this statement in your own words.

What verses or incidents in the Bible come to mind in response to this thought?

7. Read Acts 9:1–19.

How was Paul's sense of wonder developed?

By whose initiation?

What did the others with Paul see?

Why do you think they didn't see the same vision that Paul did?

8. Read 2 Kings 6:8–17.

How was the servant enabled to see the scene of wonder?

Why don't you think he had seen what Elijah saw?

9. Study the following verses and determine what they have to say about how we stimulate our spiritual senses:

Psalm 57:7–8

Psalm 107:4–9

Matthew 13:44

Luke 9:28–32
Luke 19:37–42
Ephesians 1:18
Colossians 1:25–27
Colossians 2:2–3
Revelation 16:15

Notes

1. Dixie Carter, "Brought Up Right," *Guideposts,* March 1996, 32.
2. Helen Keller, quoted in *Great Americans in Their Own Words* (New York: Mallard Press, 1990), 289–90.
3. Francis de Sales, quoted in Richard J. Foster and James Bryan Smith, eds., *Devotional Classics* (San Francisco, HarperCollins, HarperSan Francisco, 1993), 29–30.
4. John of the Cross, *You Set My Spirit Free,* arr. and paraph. David Hazard (Minneapolis: Bethany House, 1994), 59.
5. Annie Dillard, *Pilgrim at Tinker Creek* (New York: Quality Paperback Book Club, 1974), 9.
6. Amy Carmichael, *You Are My Hiding Place,* arr. David Hazard (Minneapolis: Bethany House, 1991), 84.
7. Walt Whitman, quoted in *John Bartlett's Familiar Quotations* (Boston: Little, Brown, 1980), 576.14.
8. Paul Brand, M.D., The Forever Feast (Ann Arbor, Mich.: Servant, 1993), 33.
9. Dillard, *Pilgrim at Tinker Creek,* 259.
10. Teresa of Avila, *Majestic Is Your Name,* arr. and paraph. David Hazard (Minneapolis: Bethany House, 1993), 128.

11. Hannah Whitall Smith, *Safe Within Your Love,* arr. and paraph. David Hazard (Minneapolis: Bethany House, 1992), 167.

12. Smith, "Putting the Sun in Its Place," *Astronomy,* April 1996, 24.

13. Andrew Murray, *Mighty Is Your Hand,* arr. and paraph. David Hazard (Minneapolis: Bethany House, 1994), 137.

14. Robert Naeye, "Approaching the Edge of Space and Time," *Astronomy,* April 1996, 46.

15. John of the Cross, *You Set My Spirit Free,* 46, 156.

16. Dillard, *Pilgrim at Tinker Creek,* 259.

17. Helen Keller, in *Great Americans,* 291.

18. Lucas Longo, "Who?" *Gates* 1, no. 4 (July 1976):23.

19. Hazard, foreword to *I Promise You a Crown: A Forty-Day Journey in the Company of Julian of Norwich* (Minneapolis: Bethany House, 1995), 9.

20. Helen Keller, in *Great Americans,* 291.

21. Ibid., 298.

22. Gary Wilde, ed., "An Awesome, Practical Presence," *The Quiet Hour,* June–August 1996, 4.

23. Longo, "Who?" 23.

24. Dillard, *Pilgrim at Tinker Creek,* 9.

25. Robert Burnham, "Into the Maelstrom," *Astronomy,* April 1996, 42.

26. Teresa of Avila, *Majestic Is Your Name,* 151–52.

27. Phillip Keller, "He Leadeth Me Beside the Still Waters," in *A Shepherd Looks at Psalm 23* (Grand Rapids: Zondervan, 1970), 49.

∾ *Three* ∾

KISSING COMETS AND MISSING JEWELS
The wonder of creation

San Joaquin Stroll

Drowned in a perfume sea
of spicy saps
and citrus breezes
I watch a zinc sky
summer west
across a blossomed June.

My friend's counselor advised that one good remedy for what ailed her was to get close to nature. "Get dirty, get wet, let loose, and hug a tree. Get outdoors," she exhorted.

So we planned an initiation. It began with tiptoeing across a park lawn in our bare feet and then plunging them in a cold pool. That night we read around a campfire, snuggled in sleeping bags under a full moon and clear, peaceful sky in my yard, and tangled with only one varmint: a scavenger skunk who smelled our popcorn. The next morning we made mud-pie butterflies, mushed around with finger paints, investigated the wildflowers and insects in my neighborhood, rolled down a hill, and, yes, hugged a tree.

We both felt refreshed, renewed, and a little silly, like schoolgirls at a slumber party. But we're going to do it again sometime. It was one of the highlights of our year.

We do our best to wall out the wonders of creation. We don't want to get dirty. We're too busy. We're too rigid in our routines, inflexible in our comforts. We travel, but we block out the sights with hotel rooms and motor homes. We cover earthy smells with perfumes and car fumes. We drown bird medleys with Walkmans. We become wonder-blind souls, penned behind plaster, enclosed by surround sound, sleep-walkers through life. We're like caged wild things, grown fat and lazy, who'd rather eat tidbits tossed to them than stalk the primitive hunting grounds.

Our views of the world come boxed in square screens with moving, flat pictures, dubbed with narrator transla-tions and subtitles—safely contained, neatly explained—a kind of antiseptic adventuring controlled by a remote or a mouse. Our wonder comes in copies, in replicas produced by creators whose names are in the credits.

But can these technical substitutes involve all our senses? Can they nourish the soul and spirit? Can we be more than distant spectators? Can they allow us to enter in and see through to the world beyond? Do we miss the true wonders?

What secret balm indwells a whiff of smogless air, a ray of warm sun, a strand of flowing stream, the rush of catch-ing hundreds of wrens suddenly mounting a winged charge out of a nearby cottonwood tree?

What pure oils so comprise a living outdoor pastoral scene that one noise, such as a car horn or music from a boom box—a noise barely noticed or acknowledged in the city—seems like an obscene intrusion?

Entering In

We can start where we're at: caring for a plant on the windowsill, watching weather patterns through a window slit, planting bushes in the office lobby. Those who live near nature-enhanced real estate can creep into a meadow, meander into a marsh, or venture into the deep, dark woods to meet a massive four-hundred-year-old hemlock face-to-face.

Traveling in a car shields us from wonder unless we schedule it in. A few miles outside Twin Falls, Idaho, there's a marvelous deep, narrow chasm that you'll miss in an eyeblink when you're traveling at the speed limit. There are miles of desert before it, then a sudden cutaway. Wonder seekers drive down between the granite walls to explore the bottom. I've heard there's a river and a golf course and a park down there.

Even when you're on a tight schedule, unexpected changes may provide a wonder break—if you're looking for one.

Louise and I were headed for a women's conference. But our first stop was the beauty shop for haircuts and color touch-ups. When we arrived, the stylist wrapped a cape around my neck and prepared my hair solution. I asked, "How are you doing today?"

He replied, "I've never been sicker in my life. I think I have the flu."

Louise suggested that we come another day, and he took us up on it. So, there we were, messy hair, a couple extra hours in the day, and headed for an out-of-town conference. So what did we do? Try to find another beautician?

We decided to take a detour to the Palouse Falls. We exited the highway at the first sign, followed some country roads, and asked for directions at Starbuck, a tiny town full of donkeys. We crossed a very high, very narrow bridge, wound for miles down a gravel road, and drank in the wild beauty of a gorgeous, full, roaring, rushing waterfall. The wind blew our hair. It started to rain. But we didn't care. We'd surrendered this moment to wonder.

Years ago when our family had a full month's vacation, the only way we could think of to truly get away for that long, on our budget, was to camp with our sons. We bought an army-surplus shower and tent and tin plates and ventured to a secluded campground halfway between Susanville, California, and Mount Lassen National Park. Every day was a great adventure with bugs and weather and hikes or day trips in the car and innovative recreation for a family stationed in a forest.

By the time we returned home, our house seemed like a mansion. We marveled over daily showers that didn't require a bucket brigade. We reveled in mirrors and clean faces and a dishwasher. But we missed the leisure, the intimacy with the outdoors, the challenge of making do with limited resources. We were back to the work and the hassles, but we'd had a refreshing drink of wonder.

Seeing for the First Time—Again

Nighttime and morning . . . sunrise and sunset . . . tide in, tide out of each restless ocean . . . aiming the tongue of the wagon to the North Star . . . horizons where the earth and sky seem eternally sewn together. No winter lasts forever, no spring skips its turn.[1]

These are the solid securities. These are the rock-bottom standards of what we call our world. Matthew 5:45 reminds us, "He causes his sun to rise on the evil and the good, and sends rain on the righteous and the unrighteous." Saints and sinners receive the same.

But a sense of wonder sharply awakens when we temporarily or permanently lose a familiar constant, a routine comfort. The suddenly ill or wounded or transferred know the sensation.

We're so immersed in the gifts of the ordinary that we can't see them. The rich jewels of our daily inheritance awaken in us no more wonder than the gold-and-antique-encrusted rooms of a fifty-room palace dazzle a spoiled prince. Appreciation and longing and gratefulness remain unborn until we lack something that we've taken for granted.

What if our eyes opened this morning, after a full night's sleep, but there was nothing to see? There was no light anywhere. Not a trace of the sun. No circling of stars in their firm belt. No moonshine. Not one streak of azure blue in the sky, no flaming orange or blood red or glint of subtle pink or swirls of purple. No seven-hued sweeping arc of a rainbow. No fire, not even a candle. No more lightning, that charged whip in the hand of God. Nary a firefly. And you had no idea how long this condition would last.

What if there was all the light and heat you could want and more, but no water, no moisture of any kind? You might see a few taunting clouds drifting by, but no dew-drops. Trails of mist were like a feathery, long-ago, forgotten memory. No cool cover of fog. No sweet smell or soft patter of sprinkles out of the skies. No hard-driving rain. No creeks, no rivers, no rushing waterfalls, not even a trickle. No ponds, no lakes, no rivers. No spilling, swirling snow to soften the city or powder the dusty hills. What if you awakened to the beginning of a seven-year drought?

What if there was light enough and water enough and sights enough, but the world in which you were plunged was deathly still? Not just still, but lifeless. Everything was stationary as gargoyles, rigid as tombstones. Absolutely nothing moved: not a wisp of wind, not a finch in a tree, not a varmint in the wood, not the tick of a clock, not a leaf, no human sound or touch. No jumping spiders weaving their white sticky wisps, spinning their silken lairs. No migration of monarch butterflies. No vultures circling. No volcanic eruptions, earthquakes, no grinding of tectonic plates. Sounds peaceful, uncomplicated, perhaps safer—for a brief respite. But long-term prisoners know the sheer delight they can find in the company of a rat or anything that's alive.

What if we were transferred into a world where nothing ever grew? Not a seed. Not a womb. No bursting rosebuds or wind-scattered milkweed pods. No flowers on prickly cactus. No acorns or eggs. No spindly legged calves or ponies. No yellow chick balls. No freshly drained and boiled maple syrup. No seasons, no greens, no smells of fresh cut lawn or cedar. Everything stayed the same as the day it was potted, so-called fully mature and complete, until it died, from lack of growth. No sweet homesick blooming fragrances on a summer's night. There'd be no babies. Or bulbs. Or spring.

What would it take to make water a wonder?

What would it take to make light a wonder?

What would it take to make that next bite of food a delightful delicacy?

What would it take to make the closest sights and sounds and smells and touches and movements a precious treasure?

Beauty and grace exist whether or not we will see or sense them. The least we can do is try to be there. Unfortunately, nature is very much a now-you-see-it, now-you-don't-affair. They say of vision that it is a deliberate gift.[2]

Those who are blind and regain their sight explain for us what it was like to see when we were newborns. The world's a dazzle of color patches. The colors are delightful, but other aspects of learning to see, such as the distinguishing of objects, is a torment of difficulty. The newly sighted have no depth perception, no concept of height or distance; colors and forms become confused. It's frustrating for them to realize they can be seen by others much more clearly than they can see; they may wish to close their eyes and stay in the familiar dark walls of the blind.[3]

The first time we experience a thing, we're full of wonder, but we may be seeing only blurs of color. If we aren't trained, enabled to see further and deeper, if we haven't cultivated the ability to recognize the forms and hidden images

beyond surface perceptions, we may lose the sense of
wonder. Then we'll never fully appreciate and enjoy our
world. We'll never take on the difficult assignment of
discerning the spirit and soul. We won't search out the
purpose of life or investigate the evidences that testify to the
existence of a world beyond our own.

On a starry night in 1610, in the city of Padua, Italy,
Galileo Galilei pointed his newly handmade telescope sky-
ward, stared into the eyepiece, and gasped in excitement.
Through the lens of the world's first astronomical telescope,
four white spots were clearly visible floating near a brightly
shining planet. Galileo had discovered Jupiter's four major
moons, the first (except for earth's own moon) ever seen
around a planet.[4]

What do we do after we've admired a new sight, after
we've said our "oohs" and "ahs"?

We catalog them. We write our names on the mountains
and valleys and stars we discover, as though we're the
authors, as though they're under our control, like putting a
check mark on a things-to-do list. We witness autumn in
New Hampshire, a sunrise in the Rockies, the sparkles on
the snow at midnight under a full moon on the Idaho
Camas Prairie. We watch a Sputnik launch, a man walk on
the moon; we discover new planets, stars, and solar systems
and soon settle in with, "been there, done that," when we
haven't been anywhere or done anything. We think that
with our minuscule observation we have accomplished "an
exhaustion of the secrets and novelties of Earth and of
earthly behavior."[5]

We keep wanting to probe the deeper universe, a wonder frontier. We investigate and plot the possibility of colonizing the solar system. We explore new moons. We seek some astonishing new vista to excite our waning sense of wonder, when we haven't learned all we could about the dazzling stars we already know: to appreciate their stories, to hear, as the poet says, what they're singing. We haven't yet "kissed" a fly-by comet. We're bored with the world because we think we've exhausted its store of wonders.

Everything we've seen in our personal worlds, in the expanse of our universe thus far, matters. But we've only tapped the surface of the wonders. We haven't seen everything. We don't know it all. All the wonders we think we know are but the tip of the iceberg.

Wonder happens when we reach out and literally caress a beauty we respect and admire, when we find a kindred companion who can add dimensions to our awareness, when we attach concrete to an abstract, such as meaning to a mountain. Wonder is more than novelty. It's more than thrill-seeking, although it can appear as a sudden intrusion or invigorating jolt. The merely novel, the brief thrill is totally self-centered, what makes us feel good or superior. Wonder is deeper, wider, and healthier. Wonder is bumping up against an astounding world of external glory, then reverently entering in.

Near my home lives a group of women who have uniquely combined their consecrated lifestyle of meditation with a full and practical entry into the wonder of creation. These women are nuns; they're also loggers.

Instead of habits they don hard hats and orange timber-cruiser vests. They manage almost one-thousand acres of woods adjacent to their convent. They consider steward-ship of their forest "akin to nurturing yet another gift from God" and as furthering them "in a never-ending quest for spiritual harmony in the world."[6]

While they learn the ways of the woods, they also learn the do's and don'ts of logging. And they meet God in fresh ways.

"Every day I'm finding God there," says Sister Carol Ann Wassmuth, chief forester of the Saint Gertrude's Monastery, "and learning to know and experience the goodness and abundance of God. God didn't just make ten buttercups out there. There are millions of buttercups growing out of the pine needles. God's not chintzy."[7]

Wonders Come to Those Who Wait

Photographers patiently watch for earth's most magic moments—a peacock's full plume, spread wide . . . the moon centered in a red rock archway . . . an elephant charging out of the jungle . . . a ruby-throated hummingbird feeding on a lilac . . . a brilliant electrical storm among desert saguaros . . . curtains of aurora borealis shimmering across the Big Dipper.

A perceptive observer can always find an infinite layer of wonders in any one scene. Like cloth that appears to be all the same color, closer investigation reveals a multitude of color variegations, and a Designer who meticulously wove them all together. We can become like archaeologists who spend days crouched in the dirt, digging through ancient garbage and grave sites to learn about the civilizations, the people, and the critters who lived and died in a certain place. We can search out all the published information we can find. We can walk all over an area—a park, a pond, a meadow, a city lot, a piece of desert—and write down our personal observations. The more acutely we study, the more we see.

Soil may rest as mud, inert and lifeless, for centuries. Then at the touch of a seed it becomes something new and alive.

Living soil is a community; billions of units of life.[8]

We can study the mysteries of life in an atom or in the Grand Canyon, in a virus or in a cyclone, in the forming of coal, or in asking why fossilized fish are found on mountaintops.

Daytime reveals one range of vision above our heads, but the sunlight fades out other ones. More than half the living creatures on our planet do their roaming after sundown. Only patient nocturnal observers can enter their world. At night we can poke binoculars into the heavens to scan streaking comets or falling stars or showering meteors. Or we can home in on a single star or planet. First Corinthians 15:41 tells us that "star differs from star in splendor."

We can usually see and hear more keenly at night. This is partly because the sun sends out radio waves, electronic noise, as well as light. When the sun's gone, the sky is quieter, clearer.

A World Beyond

My husband bought a small blue spruce and when he got it home he realized it had gotten terribly root bound in the nursery. "This one may not live," he warned. And it seemed he was right. The first year it got paler and seemed to shrink rather than grow.

Autumn moved toward winter, and I had been intensely concerned and in prayer for some weeks over the faltering marriage of a couple very dear to me. Heavy in spirit, I decided to get outside for a walk to free my mind of the worry. There beside the deck was the blue spruce, its stubby branch ends brimming with fresh new growth.

The wonderless scoff at "signs" like this. But I wasn't even looking for a sign. And I certainly didn't expect it from the blue spruce. However, I immediately made a connection, felt a wonderful comfort, like God was telling me that everything would be all right, that He could save a marriage just as this straggly tree had been revived. And in time the troubled marriage was restored.

Wonder develops an exceptional ear, an unequaled eye, a penetrating sense of heart.

The way the poets, the high prophets of wonder, talk about the world, they imply that everything's alive, almost human. To them, all the world's a symphonic poem. They act as if we all should hear the beating heart of every peach or see the trees composing waltzes. Or see Mars as a crimson badge, Jupiter like a reddened eye, or Neptune as "a mystic monk of frozen space."[9] Outcroppings of rocks can seem like cities set on a hill, or ships and castles or mushrooms or sleeping giants or lizards or monks' heads. Every glare of red in the sky is a fire to investigate.

Seeing nature that way requires imagination and a sense of wonder that sharpens the lens of the mind's eye. It also takes an attitude—thankfulness—the outlook that no longer takes for granted simply being alive and conveniently housed in a planet-sized garden that breeds life. The grateful approach develops through experience or enlightenment, such as surviving a mortal threat or peering into a world of truth and light after groveling in the shadows of wonder-ignorance. The questions we ask, the quests we venture out on determine our measure of the sense of wonder and our desire to cry out, "O world, I cannot hold thee close enough!"[10]

But even the nonpoet can learn to look more intensely, to see the allusions of personality in a place or created thing. After all, where else but a desert or an abandoned mountaintop would you think of burying a lonely old hermit? Or how natural to think of building a cathedral of prayer in the tall, heavenward-stretched pines.

Questions like these can help us learn to see more deeply. When we're intrigued by a scene or object, we can ask, Where can I go to learn more? What personal memories does this bring back? What historic events does this bring to mind? How would my world be different if this didn't exist? Who would enjoy knowing about/sharing this experience with me? What does this have to do with me? Is there a principle of life here? What can this tell me about God? Where did this come from? What is its purpose?

Wonder As Danger

Creation doesn't always behave. The world "is wilder . . . more dangerous and bitter, more extravagant and bright," than we suppose, with our tentative view of it.[11]

But then, some of us don't see nature as a wonder—until it's a threat. We're fascinated with the terrible beauty of nature's force, its violence, its reshaping, recreating destruction. The earth's still groaning with birth pains.

We can blissfully play on the beach while powerful winds and low atmospheric pressure brew a violent storm a hundred miles away. Soft breezes, then brisk winds, building to 140-mile-per-hour gales. Hurricane!

The longer a volcano lies dormant, the more violent its eventual eruption. Mount Saint Helens blasted with the power of five hundred atomic bombs, the mightiest eruption in the twentieth century. The creation we know can suddenly change. Entire towns, whole landscapes become obliterated. Summer turns to winter. Day turns to night.

That kind of wonder display generates gut-level respect, but it also stirs the hearty and foolish among the survivors to rise to the occasion, as though God had challenged a duel. Attempts to defy the elements may be our ultimate expression of asserting that we're somehow still in control.

We build our houses and cities on sloping hillsides and floodplains and fault lines and at the bases of volcanoes. When they're destroyed, something lures victims back to build again.

In the isolated Canadian village of Churchill, Manitoba, residents live on the direct migration trail of polar bears, the largest, most deadly carnivores in the Arctic. When they migrate, the villagers face a season of wondrous apprehension and potential tragedy. But they don't move.

And, of course, nature wars with nature.

In the jungle, three-hundred-pound lions dare to tackle three-ton hippos. Someday, the Bible says, the lion will lie down in peace with the lamb. But right now, somewhere on our world, a lion is likely devouring a lamb, ripping it apart, and glad of it.

At an antique-gun collectors show, we once saw a display of elk horns interlocked so tightly that the fighting bulls died that way—together forever. I tried to imagine the scene of the battle, the bulls trying to pull loose, the moments of realization, and the last dying breaths. A glory and a humiliation.

> The created world presents a strange mixture of beauty and horror, of splendid cooperation and savage competition.[12]

In Paul's words, "We know that the whole creation has been groaning as in the pains of childbirth."[13] Nature is a companion in the agony of our fall.

But in the mire and gore, there's also the majesty and blazes of glory and hints that this world is only a temporary wonder and mystery.

> The heavens will vanish like smoke, the earth will wear out like a garment . . .[14]

The Marks in the Clay

When we camped in Glacier Park, close to the Canadian border of Montana, the signs read: "Grizzly bear country. Stay on the trails. Make noise as you hike." So we sang and hollered as we explored the nearby trails, just in case. We never did see a grizzly. But we have no doubt they were there. We saw their tracks—huge paw prints plastered in the mud. That was indisputable evidence.

In creation, we can see the Creator's fingerprints still fresh on the DNA, His tracks on the molten lava flows, His signature on a rosebud, His shadow in a storm. But it takes the eyes of wonder. Otherwise, we see just random splotches of colors, splashes of coincidence. "I believe in Christianity," C. S. Lewis said, "as I believe in the sun— not only because I see it, but because by it I see everything else."[15]

We can see the flowers and bushes and trees all around us over and over again. They're just part of the usual, familiar backdrop of each day. But in the context of a need, of a prayer, or of a heart open to wonder, one of them could become the means of divine communication. For men of old like King David, the prophet Isaiah, and Job, knowing God magnified the wonders of creation. In the elements they saw His heart and face.

When we know the author of a book or movie or work of art we can have a more complete appreciation of the work. We know the nuances of personality, the force of character. We can hear the voice and see the face in the overlay.

When we see the Nurturer behind nature, we consider storms as possible appointed changes in plans, submissions to a higher agenda. Heaven doesn't declare the vastness of space, it declares the glory of God.

We wait. We watch. We listen—until the rocks praise Him, until we hear God sing, until He stills the storm.

Exploring the Wonder

1. Describe a time when you felt yourself completely absorbed in a scene of beauty or when you experienced an incredible awareness of nature's wonder?

What event of creation causes you wonder every time you experience it?

2. What are some impediments that keep people from seeing the wonders of creation?

What can we do about it?

3. Do you believe a person can be technologically gifted yet wonder-impoverished? Explain.

4. Read 1 Corinthians 15:40–41.

How could you discover in a fuller way the splendors of the heavenly bodies?

5. Read through the words of the hymn, "How Great Thou Art."

Which of the wonders listed in the verses, written by Stuart K. Hine, do you consider the greatest?

Do the wonders of nature ever cause you to think of the majesty or goodness of God? In what way?

6. What does nature illustrate in these passages of Scripture?

Deuteronomy 32:1–3
Job 14:18–19
Psalm 19:1–6
Psalm 23
Nahum 1:2–8
Romans 1:20
Romans 8:19–21
Colossians 1:16–17

7. If what God created is/was "good," why is it overrun with violence and destruction?

What in Scripture comes to your mind?

8. Harry Blamires says, "It is the biggest lie of bogus learning to pretend that cold common sense is against the idea of a universe designed and overseen by a divine Creator."[16]

What do you think about this comment?

Is nature more a wonder or less a wonder if it all came about by chance? If it was designed by a personal Creator? Explain your answer.

9. We're blind in the dark. Too much light can also blind us.

Do you think it's possible to be saturated with wonder? Explain.

Notes

1. Hal Borland, "Wise and Otherwise," _Guideposts,_ April 1996, 46.
2. Annie Dillard, _Pilgrim at Tinker Creek_ (New York: Quality Paperback Book Club, 1974), 8, 16.
3. Marius von Senden, _Space and Sight,_ quoted in Dillard, _Pilgrim at Tinker Creek,_ 25–27.
4. Leon Jaroff, "By Jupiter, It's Galileo!" _Time,_ 11 December 1995, 69.
5. Lance Morrow, "Is There Life in Outer Space?" _Time,_ 11 December 1995, 51.
6. David Johnson, "Sister of the Forest," _Lewiston (Idaho) Morning Tribune,_ 22 April 1996, 1A.

7. Ibid.

8. Paul Brand, M.D., *The Forever Feast* (Ann Arbor, Mich.: Servant, 1993), 57.

9. Stan Cosby, "In the School of the Planets," *Wellspring,* November–December 1980, 5–7.

10. Edna St. Vincent Millay, quoted in *John Bartlett's Familiar Quotations* (Boston: Little, Brown, 1980), 822.13.

11. Dillard, *Pilgrim at Tinker Creek,* 269.

12. Philip Yancey, "Hymn to the Polar Bear," *Christianity Today,* 17 March 1989, 72.

13. Romans 8:22

14. Isaiah 51:6

15. C. S. Lewis, quoted in "Wise and Otherwise," *Guideposts,* April 1996, 46.

16. Harry Blamires, *On Christian Truth* (Ann Arbor, Mich.: Servant, 1983), 29.

∽ *Four* ∽

TISSUES TO MEND, MONSTERS TO MEET
The wonder of creativity

Sample A: "God didn't have to explain anything. Or save anyone. He has divulged much of what He's up to, and what we've been up to, and where the celestial and demonic beings fit in, but it's highly possible He hasn't told us everything. We don't know it all, no matter how well we splice the Greek and Hebrew verbs, no matter how succinctly we explain the nouns, no matter how brilliantly we divvy up the wide sweep of historical activities into nice, neat systems. Now, if I were going to speculate on some of the things that God has kept from us . . . ."

Sample B: "K. Eric Drexler claims he has invented small, self-replicating machines that will radically transform the way material goods are produced. In the future he foresees the ability to manufacture anything from a rocket ship to tiny disease-fighting submarines that roam the bloodstream for little more than the cost of potatoes, because he uses cheap raw materials, such as air, beet sugar, sunlight, and dirt. A jumbo airliner could be purchased for the price of a car. A homeowner could pour acetone into one of these systems and an hour later, out would come a computer, a television set or a compact-disc player. A home food-growing machine could rapidly culture cells from a cow to create steak. It's called nanotechnology. Think of what this means. Why, we could . . . ."[1]

Sample C: "Keisha pushed the curtains slightly open. She squinted through the water-spotted window. No one in sight. She strained to catch a movement far down the sidewalk. She turned back to her macramé. A long, twisty bowknot hanger clung to a hook in the crossbeam of her ceiling. She pulled the strands apart and continued the twining and coiling. Five minutes to eleven. Four minutes. "What's keeping that mailman? Surely he won't be late today," she muttered.

Sample D: "If I could change anything about this world, I would . . . ."

Which of these writing samples would you be most interested in completing in your own words? Any of these exercises could plunge our minds into the wonder of creating.

Creativity is the ability to see combined with a penchant to do. But we have to look and to try more than once. We have to see with the eye, then perceive with the mind, over, around, through, and beyond, while asking a hundred related, and unrelated, questions.

The first artichokes didn't come with instructions—how did people learn to eat them?

What's the story behind Rodin's sculpture, *The Thinker?*

How would a traveler from another country, or another planet, view my daily scene?

What's God doing in our world today?

Creativity: What It Is

Creativity is what you do with what you get.

Creativity is trying to improve on something. It's the drive that transforms the thought, *This isn't good enough,* into a quest for a better way.

Creativity is talent, plus. Talent is singing or playing the notes well. Creativity is playing with the tune or writing the original notes yourself. It's honing your skills then letting fly with something crazy and new.

It's making art out of any scrap you can find.

It's viewing life from one angle, acknowledging an opposite truth, then reconciling the two. It's looking beyond the actual to the possible.

It's evaluating all we know and coming up with inventions that grow out of what we've learned, such as writing a novel about a bionic family who lives in the bloodstream of a famous athlete who is dying because of his poor lifestyle choices. How the two young sisters try to get to his brain to communicate some truths to him to save his life and theirs. About all the torn tissues they have to mend and monsters they meet and overcome. How they both fall in love with his heart, which isn't the organ but a place they fall into in his soul, a very stormy chamber that's leaking large drops of blood.

This is where they finally discover the source of his change of habits and where they meet an angel-like being who leads them into an even deeper chamber where they can choose to stay and live forever. Or they might risk their lives and the well-being of the athlete they inhabit in a dangerous trek back to their family to show them the way to the safe harbor of the deepest chamber.

A story like this is crazy, but it has an important purpose—it can start the creative juices flowing.

Creativity is messy finger paints rather than color-by-number drawings. It's silly and meaningless rhymes rather than spelling lists. It's decorating walls with crazy collages. It's spontaneity and self-confidence and impulsive notions. It's more than mastering a lot of facts or memorizing piano exercises or putting together five-thousand-piece puzzles. But it starts there. It's adding new dimensions—taking the information or material at hand and developing some totally fresh insight or product. It's an innovative, novel approach.

Thomas Hardy had it. So did Dorothy Sayers.

Johann Sebastian Bach had it. So did slaves singing in cotton fields.

Pierre Auguste Renoir had it. So did Norman Rockwell.

Frank Lloyd Wright had it. So did the Anasazi.

It's the act of putting Beethoven and a piano together to make the "Moonlight Sonata."[2]

It's seeing the architecture of Frank Lloyd Wright as frozen music or crystallized dance.

There's creativity in buttons—glass buttons with intricate details, celluloid buttons, antique buttons, buttons made in shapes of bees or cowboy boots.

There's creativity in watching the movie *Sense and Sensibility* and reading Zora Neale Hurston's *Their Eyes Were Watching God* and contrasting the themes and characters and coming to some conclusions.

Creativity awaits the igniting fires of a traveler or a poet, of an explorer or an engineer. It hovers around developers and revolutionaries. It hides in the corners of kindergarten rooms.

Creativity is gently focusing on a situation and playing with all the viable options. Creativity is passionate patience. To be creative requires a fervor for something, a buying in that perseveres: active waiting.

Creative tension evokes "a kind of conceptual elasticity that will generate new combinations."[3]

It's the ability to take up old duties and do them in a new way. It's possibilities that boggle the mind and stimulate discussion. It's paying attention to the unexpected. It's "any thinking process which solves a problem in an original and useful way."[4]

Creativity briefly suspends all the laws of the universe and momentarily embraces a lot of ideas that won't work. Creativity is taking some universal element and selecting, elevating, rearranging, associating, drawing out the patterns and putting some fresh slant on it.

Creativity is the highest level of applied learning.

The creative realize that nothing is ever wasted.

Creativity is breakthrough discovery.

Creativity is the wonder of sweat-and-strain surprise.

The Creative Process

Creativity requires that we stop paying attention to everything in order to pay particular attention to something.[5]

Creativity is a sumptuous flow, or a form of slow torture. Rarely does it come perfectly the first time. Creativity happens in stages. The questions we ask, the impractical suggestions we blurt out are the stepping stones, the provocations, the stimulations that get us there.[6]

We pay for it by going through hours of agonizing fumbling, when things will not cease to be clouded and the spiritual something we're feeling will not come clear. Creators experience long hours of birth pangs.[7]

The great creative wonders—like Bach's "St. John's Passion" and Michelangelo's paintings on the Sistine Chapel, the hanging gardens of Babylon, the treasures of the Smithsonian Institute and of the Metropolitan Museum of Art—cause our spirits to soar artfully and our minds to marvel pensively. Images out of one mind, printed and sculpted and hewn for other minds, expose a world beyond our own.

Has anything so great as this ever happened, or has anything like it ever been heard of?[8]

Creative people pay attention to their small ideas. They realize these may lead to bigger ones. And a heap of small wonders are the compost pile for an enormous glory.

It starts with a blank: a blank canvas, a blank wall, a blank paper, a blank mind.

Perhaps there's a problem to solve, a deadline to meet. In times of crisis, we become unusually receptive to new ways of perceiving.[9]

Then follows a hunch and some false starts. To create consists of doing what you have to do, your way . . . finding a flow you can follow that leads to your kind of conclusion.

The creative process is an art form and each innovator an artiste in his or her own right.

Mozart wrote the music. He may have been experiencing sorrow or joy, a season of failure or of success, feelings of love or of betrayal. But he heard the sounds in his head, recorded the notes on paper, repeated the melodies with instruments and voices.

Generations later, people can duplicate the sounds. We can hear what Mozart heard, even if we don't know how he came to hear it. Meanwhile, each musician expresses Mozart's symphony or concerto through his or her own particular personality and style.

Creativity: how does it happen?

The appraisal method

1. Slow starts, tedious middles.

Albert Einstein claimed he had no special talent, that it was simply his "obsession and dogged endurance" that helped him arrive at his world-changing ideas.

The first erector-set bridge is not always the most inventive, the first draft of a story not the most compelling. Math is learned best when we begin by counting red apples and shiny pennies instead of trying to master calculus.

Nationally known Christian poet Luci Shaw once startled an audience of would-be poets by saying, "I feel like a fraud standing up here. I haven't written a good poem in six months. I have a drawer full of abortive efforts."[10]

2. Set apart a wonder spot.

A desk, a corner table, an easy chair, a special part of a garden or park, a soak in the bathtub, a seat in an airplane—any isolated environment where you can balance rest time with work time.

Send your mind on vacation. Imagine you hear the sounds of the sea, smell the salty air, feel the Caribbean sun. You'll feel rejuvenated when you come back home.[11]

Dietrich Bonhoeffer found himself forcefully isolated, and a new form of creative release emerged. While confined to a six-by-nine-foot cell in Tegel Military Prison in Berlin in 1945, "his thinking and writing crystallized in his letters and papers, including poems, a way of reflecting his profound feelings and the depths of his prison and life experience."[12]

3. Develop a recording system.

A piece of paper, a computer, any device that can capture a creative thought. Most of us won't remember them. We must catch them when we can. They appear for a brief time, then they're gone. What we don't write down today, we may never remember tomorrow.[13]

4. Research and ruminate.

Read your favorite kind of books, study paintings and photos—anything that stimulates the mind breeds creativity. Feed yourself with music, Scriptures, and stories. Keep a journal about your world as diligently "as a musician does scales."[14] Play with all the materials at hand. Give yourself an assignment such as thinking about what to do with worn denim or used greeting cards or fallen pine cones or kids on the street.

Our brain's one hundred billion nerve cells and trillion support cells enjoy collecting data: images, words, odors and sounds, names and numbers, reasons and calculations, emotions and revelations. The left side tries to make sense of it all. The right side's ready to brood over the material, do free association, and fantasize about the options. Creativity isn't merely retrieval of bits of information; it's an active reshaping and rearranging of those bits.

> Creative people must entertain lots of silly ideas in order to receive the occasional strokes of genius.[15]

5. Let it season.

Let your brain think you're ignoring the whole project, and watch it generate ideas when you least expect it. Store what you already have accumulated and put it away. Don't look at it until you can see it afresh. It will either simmer to greatness or die a worthy death.

The mind continues to work on problems even when we are concentrating on something else. Often, the concentration gets in the way of the solution—that's why we sometimes stare. The more effort we expend, the more difficult it becomes.[16]

6. Arrive at the "Aha!" stage.

Finally, a live thought, a vibrant option has the *ping* effect. Past and present thoughts connect. The random jumble becomes a clear application to the present situation: "Eureka! This is it!" The clutter unscrambles. The precious pearl is found. The question mark becomes an exclamation point. This enlightenment may foster other impressions that culminate in one awesome projection or in an explosion of smaller related ideas.

Satisfaction resonates out of wrestling with sticky problems: making peace with a relationship, discovering a cure for a debilitating disease, finding the perfect word or phrase for a poem or letter or advertising jingle.

But creativity can be rude. It intrudes without apology—when you've just lain down after a hard day of work . . . or you're huddled under eaves in a rainstorm . . . when you're in bumper-to-bumper traffic . . . or talking with your mother-in-law on the phone. Agatha Christie confessed she got her best mystery ideas when her hands were deep in soapy dish water. Archimedes' famous "Eureka!" cry came when he solved a math problem while taking a bath.[17]

> In a dark time, the eye begins to see . . . . And in broad day the midnight comes again![18]

Creativity under pressure.

Oriental brush painting, an ancient art, requires a bamboo brush, demanding techniques, and patience to learn a most intricate, refined beauty of form. "You can't erase your mistakes from rice paper," explains Winifred Waltner.

One day she was showing one of her masterpieces to a classroom of students. "A murmur of approval rippled through the class as I carefully unrolled the scroll to reveal a graceful bamboo stalk. . . . I hung it near my desk . . . I washed my brush a few times and flicked it to remove the excess water. . . . I heard a collective gasp. . . . An arc of small gray dots covered the surface. I had ruined my masterpiece! . . . 'Lord, show me what to do,' I prayed in desperation."

She regained her composure and laid the scroll on her desk. "With my brush I painted in four more dots along with each gray dot, making a five-petal plum blossom out of each and leaving a few single dots for buds. . . . Soon a complete branch of plum intertwined with the bamboo." She hung up the scroll and the students burst into applause.[19]

Inspiration can hit like summer lightning.

Or it can fizzle like a defective sparkler. Only God can merely think or say a thing and it is done. People have to exercise their creativity or lose it.

Artist and sculptor Samuel Gore ordered something he'd always wanted—two dozen pure red-sable brushes. "I was so much enamored with these precious brushes that when I considered using them I always returned them to their box and used my old, less expensive ones. . . . After a few months of non-use, I opened the box and found that moths had eaten the brush hair, leaving only the handles. . . . The value of any brush is in its use! The sable brush, the outcome of hundreds of years of specialized craftsmanship, was dishonored."[20]

A lack of discipline isn't synonymous with creativity, a skill that must be harnessed to be used productively.[21]

The apprentice method

Apprenticeship is gaining knowledge or a skill through practice in the presence of an instructor. It's watching someone else do a creative thing. It's talking about the project with another, interacting to clarify what we most need, what will work, and what won't. It's increasing the pool of ideas by drawing pieces of the puzzle from a larger community bank.

The apprentice practices by trying to construct a model, learns through trial and error.

We become more creative when we're around people who are innovative, whether or not they major in similar interests, as long as we can see the overlapping parallels, the fascinating connections.

Our youngest son as a preschooler naturally followed the apprentice method in learning to play with Legos. For long hours he observed his older brothers putting together pirate ships and castles and whole cities. Then, he tried a few boats and houses and a car of his own, with guidance from one brother or the other. In a few years he originated his own masterpieces.

Jim excels at crafting parts for antique Winchester rifles, pieces that are no longer available. He makes screws and toggles and sights from scratch. He can make them look like antiques. He learned his tool-and-die trade from his father. But Jim's son isn't interested in carrying on the tradition. At age sixty-one, Jim finally found a young man who has the desire and willingness to learn his secrets, to whom he can pass on his skills.

We create when we have to: deadlines, assignments, problems to solve, challenges with our names on them. We become more creative the more we exercise the brain's neurons and figure out what patterns suit us, what practices energize innovation. Even the things we dread most in daily life—disruptions, disturbances, detours—can be primary sources of creativity. All the sciences and arts and technologies and even a thing called love have been improved upon because someone dared to ask, Why? What if? Why not? or How can we change this?

The Original Artist

How does God create? Where does He get His ideas? Can God alone be called a true creator? Why does God create? Is He still at it?

The God revealed in the Bible is a creative God. In fact, He holds legitimate prior claim to all ideas and inventions ever devised.

God said, "Let there be light," and there was light. All we can do is describe and define it.

From the outer fringes of the universe to the inside of a water droplet . . . from the wonders of the Venus's-flytrap to the archer fish . . . from the cold, barren moon to the watered, fertile, green earth . . . the natural world is like a second Bible. We see the footprints of God.[22]

Creating was work for God. "God blessed the seventh day and made it holy, because on it he rested from all the work of creating that he had done."[23]

God intended His creations to draw attention to Himself.

" 'To whom will you compare me? Or who is my equal?' says the Holy One. 'Lift your eyes and look to the heavens: Who created all these? He who brings out the starry host one by one, and calls them each by name.' "[24]

"The heavens praise your wonders, O LORD, your faithfulness too, in the assembly of the holy ones."[25]

God is not through creating: "Behold, I will create new heavens and a new earth." Jesus said, "I go and prepare a place for you."[26]

Unbridled creativity can be used for help or for harm, for good or for evil, for the glory of God or for the ego of man. Wisdom and motives make the difference. Wisdom was one of the first things God created: "The LORD brought me forth as the first of his works, before his deeds of old; I was appointed from eternity, from the beginning, before the world began. . . . Then I was the craftsman at his side."[27] God created the world in wisdom and in love.

Talent to create is a gift from God. It's meant to be cultivated to better the world, to improve our neighbors' lot, to bring the attention back to God. "See, it is I who created the blacksmith who fans the coals into flame and forges a weapon fit for its work."[28]

God filled a man named Bezalel "with the Spirit of God, with skill, ability and knowledge in all kinds of crafts—to make artistic designs for work in gold, silver and bronze, to cut and set stones, to work in wood, and to engage in all kinds of craftsmanship." And He assured Moses: "I have given skill to all the craftsmen to make everything I have commanded you."[29]

We partner with the Creator in copying and expanding His original works. We attempt to mirror back the wonders of creation. And as we study and meditate on the book He wrote through men, we open our minds to His direction. His thoughts stimulate ours.

The Bible is a creative miracle—comprised of sixty-six different books, written over sixteen centuries with about forty-five different authors—writers who were shepherds and kings, statesmen and priests, a tax collector, a medical doctor, and some ordinary fishermen—yet it has an astounding unity and completeness. Its pages reveal the history of humankind, the personality of God, instructions for living, and tantalizing pictures of the life beyond our own.

Jesus was a creative teacher. He used nature as a visual aid. He cursed a fig tree, drew in the dirt, made mud to heal blind eyes, pointed to the lilies and the sparrows. And He knew that everyone does not learn in the same way. He combined exposition with images, analogies, parables.

God's Holy Spirit was an agent of Creation. He hovered over the waters of the formless and empty earth.[30] The Holy Spirit works today actively helping all who ask to understand the paradoxes and polarities and seeming contradictions of spiritual truth. He stretches our minds to understand bigger pictures, to see a portion of what God sees. When God pours out His Spirit on all people, sons and daughters prophesy, old men dream dreams, young men see visions.[31]

God's creative genius is seen most dramatically in two ways:

- by saving sinners from destruction through the life, the death, and the resurrection of His Son.
- by taking any mess we hand Him and making good come out of it.

The creative attitude

"Oh give thanks to the LORD, call upon His name; make known His deeds among the peoples. Sing to Him, sing praise to Him; speak of all His wonders" (Psalm 105:1–2 NASB).

Creativity can be attributed to an individual's courage to venture out and try something new, to the grace and gift of God, and to the inspiration of the Holy Spirit. Or we can take credit for our own ingenuity and self-discipline, without acknowledging help from any other source. We can consider our talents to be self-made and self-generated, that we alone have worked for everything we've got. One stance views creativity as a source of great boasting and pride. The other gratefully counts it as something given to us for a purpose.

The creative purpose

The deepest joy in life is creativeness. To find an undeveloped situation, to see the possibilities, to brood over it, pray over it, think concerning it, work for it, to get something done there that would not have been done except for your creative soul. . . .[32]

Getting stuck is an unavoidable wedge in life. Staying stuck isn't.

Creativity caused the earliest cultures to develop tools and the wheel. Creativity undergirded the formulation of quantum theory and modern-day physics, the search for and study of black holes and superstrings in the heavens. Creativity is essential for excellence, for adventure, and for our very survival. Creative thinking makes us pioneers.

Our storehouse of literature in stories, histories, and epics—from Aristotle to Flannery O'Connor, from Homer to T. S. Eliot, from Tolstoy to the Bronte sisters, from *Beowulf* to *Gone With The Wind*—tells us who we used to be, who we are now, and who we can expect to become. Shakespeare inspires writers today. His *King Lear* influenced Herman Melville's *Moby Dick,* which helps us understand *Star Trek 3: The Wrath of Khan*. Each subsequent work draws on the imagery, rhetoric, characters, and philosophy of the former. Lear's despair and questioning of God enhance Melville's portrait of Captain Ahab even as Khan adopts the crazed poetic monomania of Ahab to justify his own doomed pursuit of the *Enterprise*.[33]

We quickly become numbed by data and historical facts. A textbook account of the Nazi murder of more than six million Jews during World War II provides us with some unbelievable and horrifying information; Elie Wiesel's *Night* causes us to see the individual lives affected and to mourn for the victims of the Holocaust.[34] Harriet Beecher Stowe's *Uncle Tom's Cabin* stirred strong feelings about slavery as she depicted the destruction of black family life by the institution of slavery. She also through fiction proposed "religious conversion as the necessary precondition for sweeping social change."[35]

Creativity provides variety, fun, diversion, enchantment. It's the romance in the humdrum. It's the touch of class in the meat and potatoes. Creativity also fixes our plumbing, bakes our bread, and gives the mattress its spring.

In 1892, Nellie Melba, an opera singer, stayed at London's Savoy Hotel and breakfasted each morning on tea and dry toast as thin as the chef could slice it. The chef was inspired to create a dessert for her after attending one of her performances as Elsa in Wagner's opera *Lohengrin*. Sculpting from a block of ice the wings of a swan, he coated them with iced sugar, then filled the center with vanilla ice cream topped with peaches and raspberry sauce. He named the dessert Peach Melba, and the crispy breakfast bread became known as Melba Toast.[36]

In 1971, Nolan Bushnell looked at his television and thought, "I'm not satisfied with just *watching* my TV set. I want to play with it and have it respond to me." He created the game "Pong," the interactive table tennis game that started the video game revolution.[37]

We need to create: to exercise our inborn abilities and make our brief lives count for something, to leave something behind that we brought into being. To create helps us make sense of our lives, makes us feel useful. It provides plans for our disorder, organization for our messes. We're more productive on the job and around the house. We're worthwhile companions for our families and friends and coworkers. We're able to make use of extra time. We never know a boring moment.

Why be creative? In order to effect change.

What worked two years ago won't work next week. Either bemoan the fact that things aren't as easy as they used to be, or use creative abilities to find new answers, new solutions, and new ideas.[38]

Why be creative? It opens the doors to wonder. Wonder is the audience; creativity, the performer.

Stunting the Process and the Wonder

The creative enter the field of competition, whether they want to or not. An accomplishment of the visionary is often plunked under the microscopic glare of comparison. Then follows the expectation of even greater achievement, thus creating competition with oneself. This either spurs the creative one on to greater works or robs him of the joys of playful conceiving.

Our greatest block to creativity is ourselves—lack of confidence, fear of our peers, lack of follow-through, unwillingness to look foolish, or a fear that what we've created is not good enough. The process of creating requires patience and perseverance and ignoring the grousers. Creative people need cheerleaders, not naysayers.

Too much critiquing, especially early in the process of creating, freezes the flow. Fear of producing something less than perfect squelches the potential for producing anything at all.

Even the masters of creativity suffered setbacks.

Flaubert, Melville, and Dostoevsky often thought their work was worthless, their lives pointless. "Had he possessed as much literary skill as wild imagination, his works might have secured for him a permanent place in American literature," said a counterpart of Herman Melville in 1885.[39] What did he know?

Creativity invites criticism or analysis of "why it won't work." Every idea, belief, and conviction forces opposition from someone who sees around the corner and across the yard an obstacle to this particular frame of thinking or plan of action. All life is confrontation and the stress of opposites.[40] But then, the best creativity often grows out of friction and conflict.

Prudent creative people learn when to present their ideas for public airing and when to keep them hidden in the safe recesses of the mind's closet. Confidence is crucial. Ingenuity can be temporarily stunned or permanently pressured into a coma by people's reactions. On the other hand, a practical advisor with no fanciful imagination at all can provide one commonsense observation that'll make the whole thing workable.

In any group of people some are ready to learn, able to create, and they will excel—because of genetics, environment, the teachers they had. People blossom in different ways, at different times. But whatever the disparity, someone admiring us, encouraging us, works so much better than the opposite.[41]

When we're ready to face the troublesome, to counter the negatives, to assess the cryptic counsel, to ignore the cynical, we can ride the waves of creative adventuring.

But too much adventuring leaves us (and everyone around us) dizzy, dazed, or dazzled. Wonder does not exist in the whirlwind of frenetic confusion or frenzied scheming.

Creating needs an ordered pace, a rhythmic tossing and turning of ingredients, a wondering it all through the mill. That's when we mend the torn tissues and imagine the monsters we'll meet.

Exploring the Wonder

1. Who is the most creative person you know?
   What is his or her most usual method of creating?

2. What's the most creative thing you've ever done?
   What has been your most surprising source of creative ideas?
   When you hear an unusual idea, are you prone to say, "That's crazy!" or "Hey, I wonder where that will lead?"

3. Exercises for fun . . .
   a. Write words that sound . . .
   - friendly
   - solemn
   - pompous
   - impetuous
   - comfortable
   - crisp

- carefree
- impassioned
- insistent
- flowery

b. Describe today's smells.

c. Describe the texture of something near you.

d. In what way is your faith like/unlike . . .
- the North Star?
- a set of blocks?
- a waterfall?
- a baby quilt?
- an eagle?

4. Give your best answer for the following what-if questions:

a. What if you were granted your greatest wish today?

b. What if you could create anything you wanted; what would it be?

c. What if mountains rose and sank every day?

d. What if, for five seconds every hour, the sun or moon didn't shine? How would this affect your daily lifestyle? Our society?

e. What if Eve and Adam never sinned?

f. What if Jesus had refused to die in our place?

g. What if Billy Graham were your father?

5. Creativity increases with motivation. To prove this consider these two scenarios:

a. A woman you once met at a flea market had suggested that the two of you "do lunch" someday. Today she calls and asks you to meet her tomorrow at the Burger King across town. However, your only car is in the shop. How will you get there?

Plan A:

Plan B:

Plan C:

b. Your dearest and best friend, who lives five hundred miles away, is deathly ill and needs your help. However, there's no airport nearby, no bus service is available, and your only car is in the shop. How will you get to your friend's side within twenty-four hours?

Plan A:

Plan B:

Plan C:

6. Describe a situation in which failure is fatal.
    Describe a situation in which failure could be very good.

7. In what way is the life of Samson (Judges 13–16) like a process of creativity?

8. The Bible is full of examples of fine art fashioned for the glory of God.
   Find at least three.

9. Has God ever had to deal with failure? Explain.

10. When and how have you ever been a recipient of God's *creative* love?
   What does it mean to you that Jesus is the *author* and perfecter of your faith (Hebrews 12:2)?

Notes

1. Gary Stix, "Waiting for Breakthroughs," *Scientific American,* (April 1996): 94, 96.
2. Marilyn vos Savant, "Creativity," in *I've Forgotten Everything I Learned in School!* (New York: St. Martin's, 1994), 97.

3. Gabriele Lusser Rico, "Push/Pull: Creative Tension," in *Writing the Natural Way* (Boston: Houghton Mifflin, 1983), 211.

4. Herbert Fox, quoted in Bill Moyers, "The Urge to Create," *Family Weekly*, 27 December 1981, 11.

5. Bill Moyers, "The Urge to Create," 11.

6. Roger von Oech, "Be Practical," in *A Whack on the Side of the Head* (New York: Warner Books, 1983), 58.

7. A. H. Gray, "Work for Joy," in *God's Treasury of Virtues* (Tulsa: Honor Books, 1995), 78.

8. Deuteronomy 4:32.

9. Rico, *Writing the Natural Way*, 213.

10. Luci Shaw, interviewed by Marci Whitney-Schenck, *Christianity and the Arts* 3, no. 2 (spring 1996):40.

11. J. Kevin Wolfe, "Six Ways to Rejuvenate Your Creativity," *Writer's Digest*, April 1991, 61.

12. F. Burton Nelson, "A Martyr's Poetry," *Christianity and the Arts* 3, no. 2 (spring 1996):6.

13. Florence Littauer, "Journalize for the Future," in *It Takes So Little to Be Above Average* (Eugene, Ore.: Harvest House, 1983), 76.

14. Pete Hamill, quoted in Bill Strickland, comp., "Keep the Words Coming!" *Writer's Digest*, February 1991, 33.

15. Marshall Cook, "Training Your Muse: Seven Steps to Harnessing Your Creativity," *Writer's Digest*, March 1986, 28.

16. Michael Seidman, "Taking the Elevator to Creativity," *Writer's Digest*, 1989.

17. Wolfe, "Six Ways," 60.

18. Theodore Roethke, "In a Dark Time," quoted in *John Bartlett's Familiar Quotations* (Boston: Little, Brown, 1980), 874.15–16.

19. Winifred Waltner, "Beauty for Ashes," *Guideposts*, April 1996, 14–15.

20. Samuel Gore, "Samuel Gore on Gore: A Sculptor's Faith Journey," *Christianity and the Arts* 3, no. 2 (spring 1996):31.

21. vos Savant, *I've Forgotten Everything*, 95.

22. Shaw, interview, 40.

23. Genesis 2:3.

24. Isaiah 40:25–26.

25. Psalm 89:5.

26. Isaiah 65:17; John 14:3.

27. Proverbs 8:22–23, 30.

28. Isaiah 54:16.

29. Exodus 31:3–6.

30. Genesis 1:2.

31. Joel 2:28.

32. Harry Emerson Fosdick, "Making the Best of a Bad Mess," in *Twenty Centuries of Great Preaching*, vol. 9 (Waco: Word, 1971), 38.

33. Susan V. Gallagher and Roger Lundin, "The Value and Limits of the Classics," in *Literature through the Eyes of Faith* (San Francisco: HarperCollins, HarperSan Francisco, 1989), 106.

34. Ibid., 112–13.

35. Ibid., 108.

36. Charles Panati, *Extraordinary Origins of Everyday Things* (New York: Harper & Row, 1987), 401.

37. von Oech, *A Whack*, 6–7.

38. Ibid., 5.

39. David Ray, quoted in Strickland, "Keep the Words Coming," 28.

40. Rico, *Writing the Natural Way*, 210.

41. Jacques d'Amboise, "Why I Teach," *Parade*, 6 August 1989, 6.

✎ Five ✎

WINDY DAYS AND SLICES OF CANTALOUPE PIE
The wonder of childhood

Recipe for: Cantaloupe Pie
From the kitchen of: Hilary Ward, age 4 1/2
    2 cantaloupes
    4 cups sugar
    9 strawberries
"Roll a big ball of all the things then smash it down. Put it in the oven. Cook for 10 hours. The oven has to be hot as the sun."
Serves: 1

Hilary explained to her preschool teacher that this recipe belonged to a Mrs. Cook City whom she visited at her "house on wheels" in Kansas. One day they had lunch together, and the menu was chicken, peanut butter and jelly sandwiches, and oatmeal for dessert. Then Mrs. Cook City asked Hilary, "Do you want a cantaloupe pie?" Hilary said, "Sure!" And then she gave her one.

Children are fun. They're also a source of trials, tribulations, tantrums, and tortures. What a wonder they are!

What if the world held no children? No nurseries, no nests, no wombs. Just mature, full-grown, properly behaved adults. Adults who'd had no childhood. Always, ever, and only. What would be lost?

Charles Dickens told the story of a boy who "strolled about a good deal, and thought of a number of things." The boy had a sister and the two "used to wonder all day long." They used to say to one another, sometimes, "Supposing all the children upon earth were to die, would the flowers, and the water, and the sky be sorry?" They believed they would be sorry.[1]

What would we miss without the miracle of babies and the exuberance of kids? On the other hand, what if this planet were peopled only by children? Imagine how that would be. How would we survive?

What It's Like To Be a Child

When the first baby laughed for the first time, the laugh broke into a thousand pieces and they all went skipping about, and that was the beginning of fairies.[2]

Childhood is much too short. There are so many woods to explore. Not just any woods, but deep, dark woods; they have to be enchanted, with thick clouds of mist swirling like an army of invading ghosts through the talking trees.

There are so many stories to read—not just any story, but ones full of magical places and winsome characters: Wonderland and Pooh Bear, Oz and Red Riding Hood, Treasure Island and Pippi Longstocking.

There are yet so many swings to soar in—the swish of the wind, the swelling dip of flying through the air, seeing over trees and rooftops into forever.

We hardly have time to explore all the new rides at Disneyland and discover all the things that we can make from Legos and learn important things like, "What do birds say to each other?" and "Where does God go on vacation?" and "Where did music come from?" And indulge in glorious silliness such as

> stuffing olives on fingers
> playing with rainbows in bubble baths
> skipping rope to sing-song rhymes
> ripping clothes on the branches of wizened
>   old trees
> constant wiggling
> tic-tac-toe in the dirt

until we're shoved into the serious games of adulthood.

Children major in opposites, noticing big cars and little feet, thick oatmeal and thin stomachs, long naps and short playtimes. They thrive on seeing patterns: circles in a shell, triangles on sailboats, diamonds in the sky.

They're fully aware of the surface underfoot: mushy mud and hard clay, cool grass and briers, puddles and crunchy snow, brick roads and railroad ties. They notice things that sprinkle and sparkle—like rain droplets and candies on cupcakes, like confetti and freckles on the nose.

The look of wonder originates in children's eyes. Simple things enamor them. Milk and cookies. Jello jiggles. Treasures tucked in corners and niches. Touching soft kitten fur. Puddles. Mom coming home.

One Nana said of her grandchild, "That little girl is either going to be a botanist or a horticulturist. She loves to explore the bugs and the leaves and all the new growth in our backyard. It was so neat to see her enthusiasm over what we have long since classified as trivial."

The seed of the adult is in the child. And the child is always still there in the grown man and the grown woman. The child in us flings up our arms while speeding downhill on a roller coaster. Or nudges us to collect things again: stamps, coins, sports cards or rocks, leaves, butterflies. The child in us lines us along parade routes and crowds us into circus tents. Or encourages us to eat raw cookie dough. Or makes us bright and cheery morning people. The child in us loves surprises.

The wind is much like a child—blowing, musing, upsetting things—mischievous, never keeping still, "always going somewhere, always doing something, always setting every movable thing in motion."[3] The wind seems to cozy up to children by the drift of soft breezes for sailing boats, for flying kites, for bouncing balloons, and for swirling autumn leaves.

A child's delight—the ones who still have the sense of wonder—is "to roam through the woods and pick up things, and carry them home, and keep them, and look them over, and classify them, and label them, and love them."[4]

Children live in a world of novelty rather than of law. They make sense of their world by wondering. "What's that, Mom?" "Why, why, why?" The child from two to five years old is the most inquisitive creature on earth in trying to comprehend its world.[5]

When we were kids we sang for the joy of singing, we colored and cut and pasted for the fun of doing it. We ran for the love of running and laughed and got scared and saw the world as a *real* place full of *real* dangers and *real* beauty and *real* rights and wrongs.[6]

Children are always concerned about growing, getting bigger, how old they are—three fingers, four fingers, four-and-a-half, five, five-and-a-half. Their growth is imperceptible to the naked eye unless it comes in spurts or we haven't seen them in a while. But it's always happening. That's the way of all the greatest wonders, like the movement of glaciers—steady, constant, year after year, then, suddenly, a breaking off into the sea.

Those who never see wonder in anything are considered jaded cynics or dried-up old codgers. Those who see wonder in everything are considered simple fools or delightful children.

Kids keep us living on the edge—of wonder.

Childhood Doesn't Just Happen

The chief characteristic of children should be freedom from care. But they also need to be warned about what happens when we're out in the sun too long, when we're too close to something that's hot, what it means to be stung by a wasp.

A child's life is one long trust: it trusts its parents, it trusts its caretakers, it trusts its teachers; it even trusts people sometimes who are utterly unworthy of trust. Famine and fire and war may rage around it, but under its father's tender care the child abides in utter unconcern and perfect rest.[7]

A child can't make it alone. Children are totally dependent. The best childhood requires the care and protection and nurturing love of grownups. In the ideal world, to be a child is to be safe. Every child deserves the sheltered space of a few years to be a kid, with protective barriers provided to absorb the threats and shocks of scaring and scarring. Otherwise we rob them, and ourselves, of the "Child of the pure, unclouded brow/And dreaming eyes of wonder!"[8]

Children are wild about playing. They need to play. Children at play are free from worry and anxiety. Playfulness is spontaneous joy, a spirit that's free. But playfulness needs the right environment: a playground they can trust, that's safe, free of ridicule, full of love. A playground protected and cared for by nurturing and caring adults.

When our youngest son was a child, we watched him in the social dance of making friends of strangers as we traveled around the country and stopped at parks. He'd run to the slide or seesaw, seemingly unaware of all the other kids, but they'd be silently sizing up one another, regarding each other by some inner sensors. Then, he and one of the other kids would run off together, as though they were lifelong buddies. They'd play nonstop until it was time to go. And then never see each other again. He could do that, because we were watching over him.

Tensions: The Generation Gap

But sometimes adults get in the way. They know too much or, perhaps, not enough. A child sees twinkles in the night sky and wonders if they're diamonds. The adult tells him,

"Stars don't twinkle. The effect of the earth's atmosphere on the star's light only makes us think they're twinkling."

A child's excited that a storm's coming. The adult stews that the day's plans are messed up.

A child wants to play. An adult wants to win.

A child sees the alphabet in butterfly wings and twigs in the forest. Adults want words on a blackboard or in a hard-bound book.

Children indomitably search for fun—in the rain, in puddles, and especially in mud . . . in the snow, on sleds . . . in the teasing wind. Adults fuss about their hair and their hats and their dress-up clothes.

A child picks flowers and ferns, collects pebbles or butterflies or snakes. Adults collect things of real value, scraps of paper: coupons, bonds, mortgages, stocks, statements.

Children are magicians, even miracle workers. They convert broomsticks to horses, toy wagons to barricades, small rocks into money, boxes into forts. They can make a game out of anything, even work and learning and the dull business of school—jumping higher, running faster, pulling harder, teasing some fun out of it. Adults tend to make work out of work and teach their children to do the same, because after childhood comes the very solemn season of real life in the real world. Not a place for kidding around.

Children at play have no concept of time. Adults constantly look at the clock.

In the mind of a child there are exciting things outside. An adult worries about sun rays, bugs and varmints, temperature, strangers, the quality of air and water.

Most children are naturally optimistic, full of the exuberance of innocence, the birthright of the young. Many adults are paralyzed with pessimism and label that "a dose of realism."

Losing It

It's hard to see the wonder while "searching desperately for a rest room with a chocolate-covered 30-pound toddler under one arm and a six-year-old making increasingly urgent pleas."[9] It's hard to see the wonder while coping with chicken pox, measles, mumps, tonsillitis, pinkeye, allergies and hair lice. It's hard to see the wonder when facing long summers with nothing to do, broken heirlooms and grimy furniture, or another season of carting strollers and diaper bags.

Children restrict freedom, increase workloads and financial strain, and generally complicate and constrain life. And the more children, the more burden. No time for self, no time alone. More separation from other adults. Stuck in the house. Decreased privacy. Harder to keep home organized, tidy.

They crowd homes and increase noise levels and stretch patience.

But children don't have it all great, either. Every child experiences childhood in his or her own way. And every generation's environment is uniquely its own.

A childhood experience depends on the climate, the atmosphere, the people who interact with the child. Are they strict or permissive? Are there two parents or one? Is he an orphan? Is she part of a large, extensive family? Are they rich or poor? What is the culture, the race? Is it wartime or peace? Do they live in the city or country? Are they wanted or unwanted? Are they taught about God or not? Are they spoiled or wisely loved?

He has five hundred dollars' worth of building blocks in his bedroom. Two dozen video games line the living room floor. Outside stand two bicycles, a basketball court, an archery target. His bookcase boasts several hundred volumes. A new puzzle and model airplane have remained plastic-wrapped since Christmas. The large-screen television pulls in hundreds of channels. The neighborhood's crawling with kids his age. How in the world can this ten-year-old say he has nothing to do? A washing machine box used as a frontier fort once lasted his father a whole summer. But the son is bored.

Games of violence. Interactive first-aid training on the computer. Toys of death and destruction. Learning to play the piano by CD-ROM. The tech mecca is boon and bane for today's kids. Glutted on Internet. Pigged out on Nintendo. Addicted to passive spectating. Our children see the world through screens and boxes they turn off and on. Today's new computing toy is tomorrow's outdated wonder.

But there's a tremendous amount of detail in computerized learning programs. Users can puzzle together the bones of a skull or peel through multitude layers of the inside of a human body—the muscles, the arteries, the vital organs. They can view actual pictures of an unborn baby at each week of development. They can explore the sky from any location on the surface of the earth (or other planet or moon) on any date and time between 4712 B.C. and A.D. 11000. Or they can see the earth from outer space and take the liberty of tilting our planet back and forth on its axis to watch the changing of the seasons or spy comets and stars and deeper sky objects in close-ups, without the inconvenience of waiting with a telescope for a particular night.

The worldwide web is a visual and audial doorway to the solar system and beyond. Our kids can space-travel anytime they want from the comfort of their homes. They can make conference calls with a dozen of their friends.

They live in the wonder of an age of gadgetry. It's like having all the wonders dumped on them at once, without the trouble of digging them out for themselves as a parceled, special kind of treasure. Wonder in other childhood eras yielded only to the hard work of discovery. Why would a child want to lie in the grass and watch the tediously slow moving clouds when he or she can fast-forward them instead?

With the explosion of technology, changes happen overnight. Everyone and everything's affected. That includes children and the childhood they experience.

Finding It Again

We can't always see the wonder in every child. But every child needs at least one significant other who will recognize and nurture its potential.

Children make winsome and useful human beings out of adults—the romping, the playing, the hearty laughs, the caring about a world beyond our own.

We learn much about a man or a woman in how they behaves around children. The first Roman emperor, Caesar Augustus, loved to descend from his carriage to join street children in shooting marble pebbles.[10]

We grow alongside children, and if we allow ourselves, we learn to freely play again and discover a rebirth of joy and delight that may have fallen asleep within us years ago.[11]

Children help us be creative: we learn the financial wizardry needed to meet expenses for the costs from crib to college.

Children help us develop endurance: the physical stamina for thirty-five hundred diaper changes per bottom, for games of wiffle ball and for mountain hikes; the mental acumen for sports stats and math games, for keeping them motivated to do homework night after night, for answering their questions, and for understanding their moods. To befriend children is like being a lifetime contestant on *Jeopardy,* but the prizes are simpler: a handful of dandelions, a sticky kiss, a crayon-scribbled "I love you" on the bottom of a homemade birthday card.

Children keep us humble. How did they behave in the church nursery? How are they doing at preschool? In the first-grade reading class? On the fifth-grade playground? Running for freshman office? On their dates? On the job? In marriage?

They also provide proud moments. The first time our son Russell presented us with an original oil painting. The time Michael, our chubby eight-year-old, chugged up

Mount Lassen's steep two-mile trail. The straight A's and perfect attendance on Aaron's high school report card.

They provide companionship. We can't jump into just anyone's life at the level of intimacy a child allows.

They help train us in the spiritual disciplines: the deeds of unselfish service, the sleepless nights when they're sick, the thousands of miles driving to and fro, the daily mission field. They provide a constant spot check on how we're developing the fruit of the Spirit. They're close enough to tangle with our weak areas where we need growth and change.

The Seed of the Adult in the Child

" 'Ah, Sovereign LORD,' I said, 'I do not know how to speak; I am only a child.'

"But the LORD said to me, 'Do not say, "I am only a child." You must go to everyone I send you to and say whatever I command you. Do not be afraid of them, for I am with you and will rescue you,' declares the Lord."[12]

We never know when the question of the moment will lead to a lifetime of research and investment.

All children have the potential to be creative in some facet of their lives—not just in the arts and sciences but in activities ranging from cooking and gardening to establishing a business.[13]

I heard of a store in Castro Valley, California. It's called "Denny's Please Touch," and it has been owned and operated by a blind boy named Denny (with the supervision of his parents) since he was nine years old. The store caters to the blind by allowing them to handle all the merchandise. Denny buys all his own merchandise, including braille scales and playing cards, talking clocks, braille Monopoly and Scrabble games, and footballs and volleyballs that beep in midair so blind players can hear them coming. It all started when Denny was scolded in conventional stores for touching everything he walked by.

Signs of adult ambitions are often displayed in childish behavior. Like the child who leaped and ran through the house and all over the neighborhood and eventually became a long-jump record holder.

"In the first grade, I remember how my enthusiasm for art got me into trouble," relates sculptor Samuel Gore. "When the new ABC Coloring Books were issued, I quickly went into action . . . then reached for the as yet unused book of the boy sitting next to me. While my parents were very expressive about this episode, they were strangely silent when, as a third grader, I charged a can of paint and a brush at the local store and proceeded to paint the back door steps and the handles of tools a bubble gum pink."[14]

Tensions: Play and Learn

A child wants to know what the dainty white flowers along the road are called, and we tell him or her how to use encyclopedias, magazines, atlases, dictionaries, and the library. A child wants to lie in the grass and gaze into the sky and watch the slowly changing shapes of the clouds, so we explain water vapor and clues for predicting the weather and how *stratus* clouds are like fog and the cobweb clouds are called *cirrus;* and if a layer of clouds makes a halo around the sun, there may be rain in the next day or so.

But we forget the poetry.

Poetry lends charm to common things. "And then my heart with pleasure fills, and dances with the daffodils" gives special meaning to the bulbs we plant together in the fall and watch come up in the spring. Playing Vivaldi's symphony, *The Four Seasons,* on the first day of winter or Beethoven's Sixth Symphony while driving through the countryside or playing Haydn's *La Poule* (the Chicken Symphony) when studying about farm animals more than doubles the learning.[15]

A child needs nourishing snacks, so we invent banana cookies, which are really banana slices. Or we play tasting games: "Close your eyes, and tell me what this is" (for a mixture of rice and broccoli). "Can you catch the airplane in your mouth?" (for a spoon of flying squash).

A child needs to learn to work, to be responsible, so we try to make it fun: How fast can you get your room cleaned? Breaking a record gets a reward.

We play Amy Grant *Loft Songs* while picking up the toys in the yard. Playfulness lightens work, enhances it, eases the stress by putting a positive face on it.

We pull science out of everyday experiences: shells from the seashore, bugs in the backyard, bird feeders in the trees, caring for a pet, digging up earthworms, catching tadpoles, hunting for caterpillars.[16] Kids love projects that leave them with something they can use or display with pride.

There haven't always been books just for children. For hundreds of years the closest was *Aesop's Fables,* a sixth-century B.C. Greek work that was translated into English in 1484. It was really a book about animals who could talk, written for adults. But children enjoyed it too. In 1657, Johannes Amos Cemenius first recognized "the importance of combining words, diagrams, and pictures as a children's learning aid," and produced a book that's the forerunner of the encyclopedia. The printing press eventually made small, inexpensive children's books possible.[17] Now there are numerous magazines and movies and restaurants just for kids.

Books and pictures lead imaginative brains into wonder. They can explore worlds through the mind that they have never actually seen. Through books they know what eastern snake-necked turtles or giant pandas look like, or the gold art and jewelry from the tomb of Tutankhamen. Or they write books of their own.

For two ten-year-old boys—Zack Roberts of Denver, Colorado, and Mike Joyer of Portland, Oregon—a fantasy became real one summer in 1988. "Me and my friend were just sitting around on the patio, and we were bored, so we just decided to write a book," said Mike. "And we were joking and laughing about would it get published after all."

They decided on a book to help kids in their relationships with their parents. The working title was, "World's Greatest Excuses." "For Kids Only," the cover read, "Top Secret."

A sample excuse for avoiding a shower: "But Mom, if I take a shower now the dirt will clog up the drain."

Mike hunted for publishers in the yellow pages of the phone book. After six calls he found an editor who wanted to expand his glossy coffee table book line into children's books. The boys' manuscript, *100 Excuses for Kids,* was released in 1990 by Beyond Words.[18]

Excuse for getting mother to buy a book at the checkout stand: "But Mom, my friend Mike wrote it."

Recitals were invented for kids—to practice performing in front of live, adoring audiences, to fail and try again, to receive applause and encouragement, to gain confidence and conquer the nerves.

> Kids coming out of elementary school may know a lot of facts about math and science, but they don't know how to apply them to any real-life situation. The purpose . . . is to teach kids how to apply what they've learned.[19]

KONOS, a curriculum for homeschoolers, encourages kids to put on coonskin caps and track animals when studying Daniel Boone, to don white wigs and write with a quill when studying Thomas Jefferson, to spend a day blindfolded and writing in braille when studying blindness. To dramatize the pilgrims, they wash their two sets of clothes by hand, clouting them with paddles in the bathtub. They sleep on leaf-stuffed mattresses, which they sew by hand. The only foods they eat are corn mush, oatmeal, dried fruit, smoked meat, and nuts.

Children learn when we put the wonder in.

The Way They Say It

"I am seven times one today."[20]

Language enables us to communicate, to explain ourselves, to make distinctions through comparisons, to hear the heart of someone else. Language happens through words, through emotions, through music, through body movements.

We begin communication with signals—toothless grins, turning away, crying, smiling, wriggling, squealing.

By the time we're four, we can say as many as four thousand words. We soak up new words like sponges, tell stories, reveal wishes, talk of real and imaginary friends. It's the golden age of language development. We may learn new words at the rate of nine per day. We begin to build complex, informative sentences, take turns in conversation, learn to listen and assess the effect of our words on other listeners. We can charm with our words.[21]

Children even play with language, with words, with ideas. They "juxtapose improbable elements, invent unlikely events, juggle semantic nonsense, all the while maneuvering in a natural sea of creative tension."[22] Adults insist on grammar and reason and logic, what's proper.

Reading stories and making up stories are crucial to children—to develop their thinking, "to make mental connections, to perceive patterns, to create relationships among people, things, feelings, and events—and to express these perceived connections to others."[23]

"Once upon a time," a saucy girl with sausage curls begins, "there were three billy goats gruff. And they wanted to get married. So they looked and looked all over Texas. But they couldn't find anyone to marry. So they built a bridge to the stars and found three mermaids. But the bridge burned up. So, they called and called on the phone, until Jack answered. He promised to make three beanstalks clear to heaven, so they could slide up them and get married. The first mermaid's name was Cinderella. The second one's name was Mackenzie. The third one's name was Snort. She wasn't very pretty. But the billy goat gruff number three loved her just the same. And that's the end, except that at the wedding they all ate green eggs and ham."

The Transition Period

The teenage years are a time of transitioning: for moving the child toward maturity, helping him or her to become fully human, caring, functional. It's a time of energy unvented . . . irresolution . . . many false starts . . . plenty of pauses and commas . . . angst and rest . . . fears and hopes for a successful outcome.

When does childhood end? When does it become a closed cadence? Is it age? Or an event? Or should it ever? Completely, that is.

The movie *Citizen Kane* is the story of a man who rose to immense power and wealth and fame but who was crippled because of the unmet needs from his childhood. But even the best conditions can't smooth all the rough places.

By their teens, many children have long lost their wonder. But there are reasons. It's hard to see beyond all the wonder-killers crowding in: struggling with peer pressure, self-identity, unfair referees, crabby teachers, fickle friends, competition and jealousy, abuse, loneliness, and raging hormones, to name a few.

In a letter, Pamela Erickson confided to me the wonder of a mother: "My daughter has entered that mysterious stage called adolescence where one day she shares her deepest thoughts and the next day dies of embarrassment because I am walking beside her. She catches me off guard with her wisdom and maturity then, without warning, closes her bedroom door to shut us out of her life. She teaches her brother how to do things ahead of his class, then torments him over something trivial."

Life is a continuous story, a mixture of comic relief and tragedy, lightness and much that's heavy. The end of child-hood is the conclusion of an act, not of the whole play.

The Spiritual Business of Childhood

Peter, a disciple of Jesus, was like a child in the wonder of seeing Jesus in all His glory on the Mount of Transfigura-tion. Impetuously, he babbled a suggestion about setting up tents, to make the moment last, to keep the experience alive.[24] He didn't want any of the wonder to leak out.

When Jesus called His disciples "children," it was a dis-arming salutation of forgiving love and hope.[25]

But we're also exhorted to "put childish ways behind" us.[26]

To be *childish* refers to the less desirable traits of child-hood—pettiness, selfishness, foolishness, emotional imma-turity, emphasis on trivial details to the detriment of important goals, infantile behavior—acts that might be pardonable in a child but are not acceptable in a grownup.

To be *childlike,* on the other hand, implies all the lovable qualities of children that transfer becomingly to adults, such as innocence and purity, faith and trust, sincerity and honesty, unpretentiousness—all the things that open more windows of the soul to let the wonder in.

Jesus affirmed kids as the key to understanding the spiritual world. "I tell you the truth," He said, "unless you change and become like little children, you will never enter the kingdom of heaven. Therefore, whoever humbles himself like this child is the greatest in the kingdom of heaven."[27]

To be truly spiritual, to be close to God, includes staying close to the heart of what kids are all about. It means keeping tuned to the child still inside of us.

A picture of the greatest peace and prosperity is described by the prophets as infants playing near the hole of cobras, young children safely putting their hands into viper's nests, or city streets being filled with the sounds of children playing.[28] A world where children can play without danger is a symbol of the ultimate perfect world.

Through children we learn compassion for imperfect people. We know their faults, and they know ours. They keep us on our knees. Most of us learn intense prayer for the first time because of kids. They drive us out of our apathy. We care when they're threatened or hurt: the wars, the poverty, the injustices, the diseases. Show us a picture of a needy, wounded child and we get involved.

Every adult needs a relationship with a kid—to help him or her grow up to be all he or she can be. Kids provide our sweetest pleasures and deepest sorrows. Getting close to kids is risky. Parenting one is downright scary.

But love and the sense of wonder and a slice of cantaloupe pie draw us in.

Exploring the Wonder

1. What are some of the interesting questions you've heard children ask?

What are some astounding observations you've seen them make?

2. What was your favorite toy as a child?
   Why was this toy important to you then?
   What is it a symbol of for you today?
   What are your "toys" now?

3. Which best describes your life environment?
   Surrounded by children?
   Engulfed in a world of adults?
   What would you change, if you could?

4. Would you like to be a child again? Why?

What scenes from your childhood do the following bring to mind?

- Incredible joy
- Deep sadness
- Quietness
- Extreme embarrassment
- Misunderstanding
- Hope
- Rescue
- Hurt or wound
- Injustice
- Freedom
- Hand-in-hand wonder

5. For mothers with children still at home:

a. Life with my children would be so much easier and more enjoyable, if

- ❏ they didn't hang on to me so much
- ❏ they weren't so noisy
- ❏ they didn't need me so much
- ❏ I could have a little more time to myself
- ❏ we had more room/space in our house
- ❏ I had more help in caring for them
- ❏ I had a friend who understood
- ❏ I got along with my neighbors better
- ❏ we lived closer to the grandparents
- ❏ I were younger (or older)
- ❏ I had help from my husband

❏ I didn't have to work
❏ I could have a part-time job
❏ we had more money
❏ I had a prayer partner with similar concerns
❏ I knew how to take care of a particular problem
❏ they would get along better with each other
❏ certain other people would be more patient with them
❏ I had some reliable person to care for them once in awhile

b. Read 2 John 1:4 and 3 John 1:4.
The greatest joy that my children bring to me is when:

c. Read 2 Timothy 1:5 and Deuteronomy 4:9; 6:6–9.
In what way have you practiced these verses?

6. Read 1 Samuel 2:21, 26; Luke 1:80; 2:40; 51–52; Ecclesiastes 12:1.
Why do you think we start life as infants, as kids?
Why not be a full-grown adult from the beginning?

7. Read Hosea 11:1–4.
How do children help us understand God as our heavenly Father?

8. Scan the book of 1 John.
   How often are the readers addressed as "children"?

9. What do the following verses teach us about ourselves?
About our relationship with God?
   Genesis 8:21
   Proverbs 20:11
   John 16:21–22
   Ephesians 5:1
   2 Corinthians 6:18
   1 Peter 2:1–3

Notes

1. Charles Dickens, "A Children's Dream of a Star," in William J. Bennett, ed., *The Book of Virtues* (New York: Simon & Schuster, 1993), 276.
2. James Barrie, "Peter Pan," in Gail Harvey, ed. *The Pleasures of Childhood* (New York: Gramercy, 1992), 9.
3. Charles Jefferson, "Fun," in *Twenty Centuries of Great Preaching* (Waco: Word, 1971), 49.
4. Ibid.
5. Kornei Chukovsky, *From Two to Five* (Berkeley: Univ. of California Press, 1963), 51.
6. Rich Mullins, "The Way We Were," *Release,* spring 1993, 46.

7. Hannah Whitall Smith, "The Life Defined," in *A Christian's Secret of a Happy Life* (Canada: Revell, 1957), 42–43.

8. Lewis Carroll, "Through the Looking Glass," quoted in *John Bartlett's Familiar Quotations* (Boston: Little, Brown, 1980), 612.15.

9. Trudy Thompson Rice, "Yo-Yos and Mountain Yams," *Arizona Highways*, June 1996, 38.

10. Charles Panati, *Extraordinary Origins of Everyday Things* (New York: Harper & Row, 1987), 369.

11. John Sandford and Paula Sandford, *Waking the Slumbering Spirit*, ed. and expanded Norm Bowman (Arlington, Tex.: Clear Stream, 1993), 97.

12. Jeremiah 1:6–7.

13. Julius Segal and Zelda Segal, "Kindle the Creative Spark," *Parents*, February 1990, 78.

14. Samuel Gore, "Samuel Gore on Gore: A Sculptor's Faith Journey," *Christianity and the Arts* 3, no. 2 (spring 1996):31.

15. Jeannette Frantz, "Science: From Boredom to Enthusiasm," *Homeschooling Today*, January–February 1996, 20.

16. Joanne Oppenheim, "Natural Science 101: Show, Don't Tell," *SmartKid*, March 1996, 36.

17. Panati, *Extraordinary Origins*, 197.

18. Fran Gardner, "Excuuse Me! We're Famous," (Portland) *Oregonian*, 1 June 1989, B3.

19. Michael Ryan, "He Makes Science Fun," (about Casey Murrow) *Parade*, 24 June 1990, 8.

20. Jean Ingelow, "Songs of Seven," quoted in *John Bartlett's Familiar Quotations*, 578.9.

21. Nan Silver, "The ABCs of Intimacy," *Parents,* June 1996, 72; Jeff Goldberg, "Yackety-Yak," 85.

22. Gabriele Lusser Rico, "Push/Pull: Creative Tension," in *Writing the Natural Way* (Boston: Houghton Mifflin, 1983), 214.

23. Ibid., 51.

24. Matthew 17:1–8

25. See John 21:5 (KJV).

26. 1 Corinthians 13:11.

27. Matthew 18:3–4; see also verses 5–6; Mark 9:36–37; 10:13–16; Luke 9:46–48; 18:15–17.

28. Isaiah 11:8–9; Zechariah 8:4–6.

❧ Six ❧

SOMETHING HEAVY, HUGE, AND HOLY
The wonder of being human

*A man is a great enough creature
and a great enough enigma
to deserve both our pride and our compassion,
and engage our fullest sense of mystery.*
Wallace Stegner

*T*here was nothing striking about their appearance. They were very ordinary people waiting for communion in church on an average Sunday.

John Fischer was a guest speaker, and he didn't know the people. "But when they filed past me down the aisle to line up in the front of the church and receive the elements," he recalls, "I noticed something. They moved so swiftly in brisk, military fashion, that I felt, quite forcefully, the wind of their presence blowing by. I felt each one displace the air around them as they took up their space in the universe."

John Fischer experienced a moment of awe as God pulled back the barrier and allowed him to see men and women, housewives and farmers—the frumpy to the balding—shine before him like "eternal beings, larger than life . . . something heavy, huge, and holy."[1]

He caught a rare, "other world" glimpse of human beings—the glory of their significance, an inkling of God's image in them.

The Wonder of Who We Are

There are no insignificant people.

I know that. I'm very aware of my existence. I may not be the greatest, the smartest, the wealthiest, but I'm not insignificant. I have thoughts. I have feelings. I own a custom Texas conversion Suburban, therefore, I am. I have a life. I'm the most significant person I know—to me.

There are no insignificant people.

This idea isn't too hard to accept, if I limit this precept to a few select folks—compatible family members, cherished friends, notable folks in the news. But, everyone? The strangers who roar past me on the highway? The hordes in the crowd scenes who wave from the stadium on ESPN? The barefoot, dirty-haired, garlic-breathed woman in the post office?

There are no insignificant people.

Wait a minute. What about the scumbags in this world who'd sooner shoot you than give you the right-of-way, who'd rather steal your last ten-dollar bill than give you the time of day? What about lazy bums? And scatterbrains? And people who are just plain, you know, s-l-o-w. What about the folks whose only reading is the tabloids, who consider laughing at sitcoms a form of aerobics, who spew hollow thoughts in holy places?

There are no insignificant people.

But I don't have to care equally about them all, do I?

Not if you can't see the wonder. But still, *there are no insignificant people.*

Significant in what way? And to whom?

C. S. Lewis saw people as John Fischer experienced them for a brief moment on a Sunday morning. Lewis wrote: "It is a serious thing to live in a society of possible gods and goddesses, to remember that the dullest and most uninteresting person you can talk to may one day be a creature which, if you saw it now, you would be strongly tempted to worship, or else a horror and a corruption such as you now meet, if at all, only in a nightmare. All day long we are, in some degree, helping each other to one or other of these destinations."[2] There are no ordinary people. Your neighbor is the holiest object presented to your senses.

We can think about ourselves too much: who we are, what we aren't, how great, how horrible, how full of potential. But we can never think too often and too deeply about the welfare and potential and well-being of those around us—about the wonder *they* are. The value that's placed on human life is the litmus test of character and soul for an individual, a society, or a nation.

Think, if you can, of someone you once knew who seemed dull and quiet and without a ray of talent or genius yet much later in life became a renowned architect or the founder of a diamond mine in the desert or a diplomat who mediates peace in the Middle East.

Or recall a teen who was surely destined for a life of barhopping or drug-dealing or prison or some other dead end but instead became a dedicated missionary in Uganda or is finding a cure for rheumatoid arthritis.

Somewhere along the way, a light turned on. These people found something worth living and dying for. In the early days their minds were darkened, their passions untamed or undirected, their wills unleashed. But change intervened. And all who see it are filled with wonder.

Those with a well-developed sense of insight will see the potential, long before the turning.

"You judge by human standards," the Scriptures scold.[3] But even by human standards, what a wonder we are!

Sense Ability, the Body Works

Science has helped us unveil the wonders of the human body.

Each body contains thirty trillion cells that reproduce themselves every seven years. Each one of these cells performs ten thousand different chemical functions.

The heart is a complex device that beats more than 2.5 million times during an average life span.

The hand is so dextrous it can perform as many as fifty-eight different movements with seventy separate muscles.[4]

Our eyes "perceive the world with a third dimension that lets us walk through the forest without hitting the trees."[5] From the top of a mile-high mountain—with no obstructions on a clear day—someone with normal vision could see a distance of about ninety-six miles.[6]

Crammed into our skulls are "as many neurons as there are stars in the Milky Way." Each neuron receives input from about ten thousand other neurons in the brain and sends messages to a thousand more. The combinations possible are staggering.[7]

The human brain is a three-pound organ that "continues to elude comprehension and defy imitation. . . . [It's] the most complex thing we have yet discovered in our universe."[8] It sees images and remembers them. It collects words, names, numbers, odors, tastes, and sounds. On command, it moves legs, arms, and fingers. It can read, write, reason, and calculate.[9]

The senses of taste and smell "must still be rated as the chemical masterpieces" of our bodies, and the olfactory cells are "some of the most amazing chemical laboratories on earth."[10]

And like fingerprints, the iris pattern in each person's eyes is unique.[11]

Our skin, "a seamless body stocking," is a vital, humming source of ceaseless information about our environment; it's studded with half a million tiny transmitters and functions chiefly as a waterproofing barrier that keeps the inside in and the outside out.[12] It provides a defense against bacteria and various critters as well as blows and bruises to the organs. Our skin is "tough enough to withstand the rigorous pounding of jogging on asphalt, yet sensitive enough to have bare toes tickled by a light breeze.[13] There are 450 touch-sensitive cells in every one-inch-square patch. Part of the essence of what it is to be human is contained within our skins.

The bloodstream functions as an efficient, incredibly fast-working whole-body processing plant, sorting and filing nutrients and waste products, with specialized cells equipped to eat bacteria.

Simple breathing requires cooperation of ninety chest muscles.[14] What a responsibility, what wisdom is needed to properly feed and care for this incredible organism!

Through our bodies we have the ability to experience what it feels like to be *alive*. When we stand under the rush of a waterfall, when we stick a big toe in a tub of hot water, we feel a sudden realness, a knowing that we exist, the novelty of being who we are: "You feel life wipe your face like a big brush."[15]

Sense, the Windows of Soul and Spirit

What an insignificant part of a person's life are his acts and his words! His real life is led in his head, and is known to none but himself. All day long, the mill of his brain is grinding, and his thoughts, not those other things, are his history.[16]

The body is the physical part of us that is connected with and encloses another living part of us that we can't see or touch.

The soul is the self, the personhood, what it means to say *I*, the center of thinking and feeling and the will. The spirit is our spiritual inclinations, our moral sense. To our natural observance, these qualities are so meshed and overlapped it's difficult to separate them. Only "the word of God" claims to be able to penetrate "even to dividing soul and spirit, joints and marrow."[17] Within the soul, within the spirit of a human being, lodges all the other senses, giving the ability to

- detect something's wrong
- wonder what's missing

- celebrate a victory
- see another's point of view
- acknowledge our faults
- feel compassion
- burst out in laughter
- express sincere praise
- expand the mind
- enlarge the heart
- purify our motives
- have visions and dreams
- want, desire, express passions, swell with zeal
- fear death
- be crushed by sorrow
- be empty and lonely
- smell an adventure
- touch this world with the reverence due the next
- seek truth
- enjoy goodness
- change
- develop a well of wisdom
- seek and find God

If we were bodies only, we'd be robots, computerized wizards, mindless brains. Some believe that's what we are. "But even people who believe they are machines cannot live like machines, and thus they must 'leap upstairs' against their reason and try to find something that gives meaning to life, even though to do so they have to deny their reason."[18]

The soul and spirit provide that disarming charm (or pricking pain) we call personality.

Our Being

We're an irony.

We vacillate. At times we grab the nearest pleasure, no matter what the cost, because this moment is all-important. At other times we single-mindedly venture as close as possible to God, recognizing Him as our primary source of deep satisfaction now and of glorious rewards in the hereafter.

We cause dilemmas. We're unruly, rebellious. We dabble in cardinal no-no's. We're sucked into addictions. Yet, we're being trained to rule over future kingdoms.

We're in a quandary: "we live under two orders, we are at once a citizen of Eternity and of Time,"[19] and we must learn to assimilate and balance the two: the spirit and the soul, the earth and heaven, living and preparing to die.

We're paranoid. We have a penchant for being seen. But we also want to tuck into ourselves like cocoons, all curled up and hidden from everyone. Even God. We have this feeling that someone's watching, even when we're alone. Sometimes it's a scary kind of peered-at feeling, like in the middle of the night. But most times it's a quiet, benign, friendly kind of knowing that there's a witness or two, that our lives are being played out before an audience. And we wonder if they're friend or foe.

We admire a virtuous man, a rational woman, an industrious teen. We despise the idle jester, the quarrelsome fool, and yet we're prone to act both.

We're incompatible with our belief systems. We're nice, but not many are noble. We're smilers, but not many have great souls. We're wounded warriors with a patented victory cry. We're godly saints with a raging temper problem. We're a fractious lot lifting a unity banner.

We're a glory—awakened to life by God's breath, a housing for His majesty, the crowning achievement of creation, and we're the only creatures who'll stand before the final judgment seat.

We're lovers of purpose and of pleasure, with the freedom to choose. We're prone to pride that sometimes overlooks decency. We're sensitive souls who can be reckless. We're survivors with a tinge of arrogance. We're loners looking for kindred spirits. We seek all-inclusive theorems for life after failing bonehead math. We think we see, but we're sound asleep. We're "always learning, but never able to acknowledge the truth."[20]

We're born. We grow. We learn to fly . . . or sing . . . or rail against prison walls. We cry out in joy, in pain, in grief. We constrict our hearts or widen our souls. Some do what they're here for. Then, we all die.

The hardest thing to do is see ourselves as others see us or perceive another person's point of view. We can exaggerate our fears or our confidence and come to false conclusions.

Life kicks against our hearts, rubs against our souls, quickens our spirits. Joy here is hard-won, but possible.

And wherever we go, there we are, and so are they: the teeming, milling, intruding others.

> What is a house but a bigger skin, and a neighborhood map but the world's skin ever expanding?[21]

Our planet's an enclosed community and we're all beating hearts with a part to play in the universe.

Our Doing

Penned by a man from a refugee camp:

> Son, do you know that I dream? . . . Without a dream, what kind of future would you have? . . . . I dream that we will have a secure shelter, a house with a thickly woven roof (better yet, metal!) and strong mud walls, cool in the heat and dry in the rain, a home among the trees above the flood waters. I dream of a strong pair of oxen and a field to plow. . . . Sometimes I am afraid to dream. What is a father to do? But for you, my son, I will still dare to dream.[22]

From the storefront streets of Harlem to the ivory towers of Princeton, from the magnificence of Sanskrit to the manufacture of Hondas and Yamahas, from the graffiti in cave dwellings to the skyscrapers of New York City, we have abilities and aptitudes that far exceed those of other creatures. An animal sees what's in front of its nose. Human beings view the universe. We dream dreams. We fancy visions. We're able to aim for goals, to apply our efforts to some good end.

Wrote Booker T. Washington, the former head of the Tuskegee Institute of Alabama and an outstanding American public speaker and writer: "I was born a slave on a plantation. I am not quite sure of the exact place or exact date of my birth, but at any rate I suspect I must have been born somewhere at some time. . . . My life had its beginning in the midst of the most miserable, desolate, and discouraging surrounds. . . . Of my ancestry I know almost nothing. . . . I had no schooling whatever."[23] Yet, he excelled far beyond his meager origins.

We invent gadgets for our comfort and glittering amusements that waste the soul. But we can also discern priorities, the kind of thing that drives us to sacrifice ourselves in obscure places.

We're walking down the street, utterly worn out from a long, hard week. We're so tired we'd gladly sprawl on the ground to get some sleep. Suddenly, there's a cry. There's been an accident. A child's hurt. We rush to help. And never remember how exhausted we'd been until the crisis is over.

Albert Schweitzer, a scholar, a theologian, a lecturer, and a superb musician, Europe's master organist, chucked it all to become a mission doctor in Africa. When he had performed his first operation and brought a black bundle of suffering humanity back from the brink of death, he exclaimed, "I wish my friends everywhere but knew the exquisite joy of an hour like this!"[24]

We're able to acquire common knowledge, the accumulation of wisdom and insight of other people through the ages, through oral histories and books, learning through the experiences—the failures and successes—of those who've lived before us. We don't have to start from zero every time a new generation's born.

Masterpieces are not single and solitary productions; they are the outcome of many years of thinking in common, of thinking by the body of the people, so that the experience of the mass is behind the single voice.[25]

We design. We organize. We think, therefore we do.

Some people said, "Humans will never fly." The Wright brothers didn't believe it.

Growing peas is a very common activity. But when Gregor Mendel crossbred them in a monastery garden he discovered patterns that led to new perceptions about the principles of heredity.

Everybody else looked at the woodblock printing on playing cards and raised their bids or asked for another deal. Gutenberg looked and thought of movable type—and the printing press.[26]

We cut Mount Rushmore into faces.

Louis Pasteur isolated the bacillus in a disease of silkworms and established the germ theory that produced a lifesaving vaccine.[27]

Construction of the Panama Canal required ten years, twenty-thousand workers, $336,650,000 and the moving of 240 million cubic yards of dirt.

Great works. Monumental tasks. Mind-boggling challenges. Dedication. Giving everything for a worthwhile cause. Birthing great ideas. Then someone must invest grinding years at dull tasks to fulfill the vision.

A former opera singer, Deforia Lane, dedicates her talents to using music therapy to treat critically ill patients—with astonishing results.

Kay Cole James, tempered by adversity and discrimination but nurtured by a strong Christian mother, rose from her lean childhood in a poverty-stricken family to her appointment in the executive branch of the U.S. government.

Then, there are the great communicators, with the "ability to show us the world anew, to educate and entertain us, to change the ways we think about ourselves and others," the broad, sweeping ideas and inspirations that influence wide audiences.[28]

People of the twentieth century have witnessed more change than any people who ever lived: from the century of steam to the century of oil and electricity; from the age of the computer to the age of genetics. Our ability to generate wonders seems multiplied.

All told, genetic technology will give humankind an almost godlike power to improve its condition. It will be one of society's major tasks in the twenty-first century to develop a moral and ethical code to match and help control this awesome ability.[29]

In Heaven's Eyes

"I have engraved you on the palms of my hands."[30]

People. Our life-giving planet. The lifeless universe. Which is the greater wonder? Without humanity the world would be unfinished, incomplete. We bring order, structure, and beauty as our distinctly human contributions to this world. We offer our wonder and awe as responses to the incredible environment created just for us.

We're part of creation. We're answerable to the Creator. We're stewards of our world. We have a highly exalted status.

"What are we made for? To know God. What aim should we set ourselves in life? To know God. . . . What is the best thing in life, bringing more joy, delight, and contentment than anything else?" Knowing God.[31]

If we don't, we return to the jungle. We fail in our essential purpose. We fail to be human. We could say that the human race is a great coauthorship in which we are collaborating with God and nature in the making of ourselves and one another.[32]

He made us for Himself, for His enjoyment and ours. He uses us to accomplish His purpose. We're *His* offspring.

We have bodies. We have souls. We have spirits that can be cultivated or lost. With them we can interact with God, we can grow, we can change. Every man and woman, boy and girl, who has breathed on this earth—regardless of race, nationality, color, rank, or social condition—has infinite worth. Each person who leaves this earth produces a void no one else can fill.

Why do we find this so hard to believe?

For one thing, there are so many people. The numbers stagger the mind and bind the heart. If there were fewer, would we find each one more valuable? Would life for everyone be more rewarding? Can only God love in millions as well as in ones?

For another, there are evil people, with warped and callous motives and seared consciences. At times, even God has felt He created a monster He wanted to destroy.

However, we're awakened to wonder when some event, some imperceptible moment, after many events of time have passed, causes us to really see another person for the first time. We blink. We're startled. We see something we never saw before. We catch a glimpse of his value, her worth. We recognize the image of God. We feel God's presence in someone's laugh, someone's prayers, someone's sacrifice. We see more than shape and appearance, more than skin and bone, more than face and body. We see into the soul.

Exploring the Wonder

1. What gives you the deepest pleasure in life?
   What is the most enjoyable part of today for you?

2. What does our world need more than anything else?
   What do you need more than anything else?
   What does your neighbor need more than anything else?

3. What do you think is the great divine purpose in creating humanity?
   How do you feel about the possibility of finding life on other planets?

4. Who are the kind of people you admire the most? The least?

5. Describe a time when your view of the worth of another human changed completely.

6. Do you believe that you have done or are doing what you were created for? Explain.

7. What do you understand to be the ultimate meaning of life?

8. Read 2 Samuel 23:15–17.
   Why do you think David refused to drink the water? Do you agree with his action?

9. Harry Blamires wrote: "The Christian mind surveys the human scene under the illumination of the fact that God became man, taking upon himself our nature, and thereby exalting that nature for all time and for eternity. Thus the Christian's conception of the human person is a high one, his sense of the sacredness of human personality being deeply grounded in revealed theological truth."[33]

How does the fact that Jesus was God in human flesh increase your wonder of being human?

10. What do these verses imply about the wonder of being human?

Genesis 1:26–27, 31
Genesis 2:7
Genesis 5:1–3
Genesis 9:6;
Leviticus 24:17
Psalm 8
Psalm 139
Proverbs 14:31
Isaiah 45:12
Jeremiah 1:5
Matthew 10:30–31
Acts 17:25–27
1 Corinthians 15:42
Colossians 3:10
James 3:9

Notes

1. John Fischer, "The Shining Ones," *Moody*, November 1994, 30.
2. C. S. Lewis, *The Weight of Glory and Other Addresses* (New York: Macmillan, 1980), 18.
3. John 8:15.
4. Paul Brand, M.D., and Philip Yancey, *Fearfully and Wonderfully Made* (Grand Rapids: Zondervan, 1980), 163.
5. Harold Sala, "Man Is Wondrously Made," *Guidelines for Living*, April 1996, 11.
6. Roberta Kramer, ed., *A Book of Curiosities* (Middle Village, N. Y.: Jonathan David, 1975), 22.
7. J. Madeleine Nash, "The Frontier Within," *Time*, special issue, fall 1992, 81.
8. Ibid.
9. Earl Ubell, "The Brain Reveals Its Powers," *Parade*, 13 September 1992, 20.
10. Paul Brand, M.D., *The Forever Feast* (Ann Arbor, Mich.: Servant, 1993), 30–31.
11. Karla Harby, "A Discerning Eye," *Scientific American*, (April 1996): 38.
12. Brand and Yancey, *Fearfully and Wonderfully Made*, 14, 152.
13. Ibid., 124.
14. Ibid., 188.
15. Annie Dillard, *An American Childhood* (New York: Quality Paperback Book Club, 1987), 249.

16. Mark Twain, "Autobiography" (1924), quoted in *John Bartlett's Familiar Quotations* (Boston: Little, Brown, 1980), 626.9.
17. Hebrews 4:12.
18. Francis A. Schaeffer, *How Should We Then Live?* (Old Tappan, N. J.: Revell, 1976), 166.
19. Evelyn Underhill, quoted in Richard J. Foster and James Bryan Smith, eds., *Devotional Classics* (San Francisco: HarperCollins, HarperSan Francisco, 1993), 113.
20. 2 Timothy 3:7.
21. Dillard, *An American Childhood,* 44.
22. Jon Warren, "A Father's Dream," *World Vision,* June– July 1996, 15.
23. Booker T. Washington, quoted in *Great Americans in Their Own Words* (New York: Mallard Press, 1990), 247–50.
24. Albert Schweitzer, quoted in Frederick Brown Harris, "Spires of the Spirit," *God's Treasury of Virtues* (Tulsa: Honor Books, 1995), 266.
25. Virginia Woolf, *A Room of One's Own* (New York: Harcourt Brace Jovanovich, 1957), 68–69.
26. Bill Moyers, "The Urge to Create," *Family Weekly,* 27 December 1981, 11.
27. Dillard, *An American Childhood,* 107.
28. Jim Clark, "He Remains One Visionary Leap Ahead," *Time,* 17 June 1996, 54.
29. Leon Jaroff, "Seeking a Godlike Power," *Time,* special edition, fall 1992, 58.
30. Isaiah 49:16.

31. J. I. Packer, "Knowing and Being Known," in *Knowing God* (Downers Grove, Ill.: InterVarsity Press, 1973), 29.
32. Wendell Berry, *Home Economics* (San Francisco: North Point Press, 1987), 115.
33. Harry Blamires, *The Christian Mind* (Ann Arbor, Mich.: Servant, 1963), 156.

ᔆ Seven ᔆ

THE AGONY AND THE ECSTASY
The wonder of loving

Last night I lay awake and thought of all the inhu-manity of it, the beastliness of the war. I remembered all the brutal things I had seen since I came overseas, all the people rotting in jail, some of whom I had helped to put there. . . . And this morning when I rose, tired and dis-traught from bed, I knew that in order to survive this time I must love more. There is no other way. (An entry from the journal of an American soldier.)[1]

Like this soldier, we're often overwhelmed with oppres-sive events beyond our control. Love isn't easy in the car-nage of daily warfare either. The biggest challenge of life is knowing how to do it better.

> *It burns like blazing fire,*
> *like a mighty flame.*
> *Many waters cannot quench love;*
> *rivers cannot wash it away.*[2]

The *Summum bonum*

There are so many different kinds of love, so many ways to show it.

Duty packs a sack lunch. Love slips in a surprise. Obli-gation sends children to bed. Love tucks in the covers.

Responsibility vacuums the carpet every day. Love covers the family with prayer. Manners pours a glass of milk. Love adds the chocolate and marshmallows.[3]

Love is above all things, the greatest of gifts, the first of the fruit, the difference between life on earth as a living hell or as a blissful taste of heaven.

What is this thing called love?

American artist and author James Thurber told of a forty-seven-year-old woman who had been married twenty-seven years and had six children. Out of the nitty-gritty of her daily experience, she had her own definition: "Love is what you've been through with somebody."[4]

It takes lots of stuff intervening over the contours and contexts of time and purposeful action, and an object of our affections, to make love. We never do it alone. Love doesn't ignite in isolation.

Love is a flame and a cool breeze. Love is a flood and a welcome trickle. Love is ecstasy and torment. Love is freedom and slavery. Love is a prize and a prison. Love is strange and sacred. Love is patching and sealing a neighbor's driveway or bringing a fresh-baked apple pie.

Love is yanking a knife away from a child, gently wiping crumbs from Grandma's face. Love is a van full of women traveling six hours round-trip on a hot, humid day to visit a friend in the hospital.

Love is a touch on the shoulder, an embrace in the park, making love between the sheets. Love is the tender passion. Love is power, and powerful love is a gift, but only if we receive it.

Love is heated discussion with a safety net. Love is polite warfare. Love is insatiable tension. Love burns deep. Love is the dog days of commitment, the white flag of compromise, the roughhouse of communication. It's the kinder, gentler battlefield.

Love is "a palpitating, quivering, sensitive, living thing. . . . Love is an effect,"[5] an aftermath, a consequence, the result of hundreds of actions. It's critical, yet it's a crazy bit of nonsense. It requires blood, sweat, and tears, yet it's like magic. It's solid yet illusive. The more we study it, analyze it and categorize it, the more mysterious and preposterous it seems.

Defining love is akin to nailing Jell-O to the wall. When you think you've got it nailed down, it slips and slides away from you.[6]

The spectrum of love is wide and full and long. Love is cherishing and charitable, caring and cordial, captivating and considerate. Love is a carefully crafted note sent to the lonely man who gets no mail. Love is bear hugs and back rubs. Love is strong, strange longings inside of us. Love is complicated and straightforward, puzzles and contradictions, tit for tat, selfishness and self-giving, all at the same time. Persistent love is a primitive emotion that can soften the jaded sophisticate or conquer a cranky old codger. Love is sometimes maudlin and mawkish, other times serene and sublime. Love is smiles and a place where we're needed— and wanted. Love helps us find our way back home.

But even at home people can be hard to love.

Love is an encouraging atmosphere among the faults, an attitude of "let's try again," a decision to overcome the antagonism. To love only one other person does not a lover make. Love is a lifestyle. Love is the difference between profound humanity and superficial existence. Love is full acceptance, no strings attached, with an eye to growth. Love is not indifferent or hostile, aloof or chilly. Love is the ability to rejoice in another's success, to weep in another's failure.

Love can be tough or manipulative. It can be unconditional or bought with a song. The best of music and the worst of music was composed in the name of love. Love starts with an invitation to know and be known. It's saying, "Come on in. You are important."

Love means spending hours to interpret meanings, to think out loud together, then "riding the planet like a log downstream, whooping."7 It's the making of soul mates.

The wonder of love, after all the betrayals and bitterness, disappointments and cynicism, is that it still happens. A family burned out with the trials of foster parenting vowed never to be taken again—until they were drawn into those deep, dark, sad brown eyes.

The wonder of love can be given by anyone, in the most surprising manner. A man, despondent to the point of suicide by the sudden death of his wife, slumps against a streetlight after a long, aimless walk through the bawdy side of town. A lurching drunk bumps him. The man pays him no attention. The drunk looks him over, then in one lucid moment says, "She's gonna be all right. Yessir, she's gonna be all right." The drunk tucks a dollar bill into the despondent man's hand and stumbles down the street. The man ponders the scene, gathers his wits, marches home, and gets on with life.

The wonder of love—we can have it with or without feelings. But the feelings can be stirred—what if this drunk were my own son? What if that druggie were my own daughter?

The wonder of love—it can bring so much hurt. We now know that the heart of Prince Charles belonged to Camilla before he married Diana in the most glamorous, most-watched wedding of the century. Love is always risky. If we want to be assured of never having our hearts broken, then we must never love anyone or anything. There can be no estrangement if there has been no connection, no affection. But when hearts are locked up, safes turn to caskets.

The wonder of love—its best work is done in secret. In fact, the more public the display and noise, the more it becomes something other than love.

The wonder of love—it gives us a different focus. Some love lepers. Others love criminals. Some love the dying people of Calcutta. Love disposes rulers to rule justly, seriously, faithfully. It's at the heart of every decent and good human act. It's the very being of God. We all have our people to love.

Love is good for us, good for others, good for society. It's life's most powerful influence, affecting everything we think and do. But love is a very private choice. It's an act of the will. We either want to, or we don't. We either try, or we bail out. We make the leap, or we decline to enter in.

It's easy to talk about love but so hard to live it, to stay there in it—past two years, through ten years, on to twenty-five years, into gold-medal wear-and-tear-and-care years. Still holding hands after all those tears. That kind of love begins by making an awesome promise and keeping it. Love is not for the lazy. But those who climb high mountains and survive don't complain about the view on top.

Love is a lifetime work of art, art in motion. Love lasts forever. We can take it with us.

The Chemistry of Cuddling

The soul. The body. The real world and dreamland. The prodigal's father and the Song of Songs. Poetry and phenylethylamine. The imprint of love is a comingling affair.

Cascades of neurochemicals, which serve as natural amphetamines, flowing from the brain to the bloodstream produce feelings of euphoria and elation when there's romantic attraction. Stronger and longer bonding, head-over-heels and crazy-in-love feelings can be traced through the larger amounts of endorphins, chemically similar to morphine, that flow into the brain. The brain's pituitary gland secretes oxytocin, which stimulates sensations during lovemaking and produces feelings of relaxed satisfaction and attachment.[8]

It's what happens when couples interact—the facial expressions, the heartbeats, interpreting one another's emotional cues. The chemical pathways are the same as those found during high stress. This explains the physiology of love.

But love has many channels, many recorders, numerous outlets. Love comes in a variety of types to accommodate a gamut of relationships. We need more words for it.

It's the adoration of devotion, the lifelong coach weeping for joy in the corner. It's the infatuation of eros, the caressing of a lover. It's cherishing a sweetheart, ambling arm in arm. It's the esteem of admiration, the respect and companionship of *philos,* a morning jog on the same levy path, the understudy joining in the applause, going the third mile.

It's something we relish, a passion we savor. It's the kindness of charity—running a marathon for the Red Cross, providing the picnic baskets, underwriting the production.

It's the sacrifice of agape, love's mad self-forgetting, traced on the form of a crossed tree. A man pouring out His life's blood for His friends. An innocent's death, while the guilty go free.

Any love can sour, can be corrupted. Any love can take a higher road, when it determines not to injure any human soul or degrade any human spirit. To love is to enlarge the soul. To withdraw love withers the heart.

When we bypass the soul and spirit in relationships, when we're too familiar with sex—let it intoxicate us too young and too early and with too many—we lose its mystery and wonder. When we don't wholeheartedly commit to one partner and the lifelong work of love, we become "flat-souled . . . unadorned by imagination and devoid of ideals."[9]

The challenge of relationships gives us much to look forward to, much yet to grow up to, keeps us fresh and immersed in innocence because there's so much left to know. Relationship is a gift; it's also learned.

However loved we might actually be, we may not feel loved until there is some touch or time given or some act of service or special gift given or the timely and sensitive word spoken. Love isn't done with computers. It's earthy work. It's watering and planting and digging down in the dirt and mud and tending the delicate roots. It's get-real-and-pull-the-infernal-weeds kind of work.

Love: What It Does for Us

> No worse fate can befall a man in this world than to live and grow old alone, unloving and unloved.[10]

This life we live that thrills us, that torments us, that sometimes bores us, is so closed in around us. It's barely noted by anyone else. To have some other person notice our existence, really notice, and nod a signal of communication, of recognition, that's a wonder. To have someone lean in and touch the soul and whisper, "This is forever, you and me," that's a greater wonder. Love blesses a day, a moment, a life.

In the wake of love the soul is "stripped of its own small and self-centered ways of looking at the world, stripped of the strengths by which it tries to shape everything and everyone to its own will."[11] We need people if we are to know anything, even ourselves.

A couple of high school chums get together for a reunion lunch, and in a moment of honest sharing one will say, "I never knew how selfish I was until I got married. I never knew how angry I could get, how ugly I am, until I became a parent."

Truth becomes clearest to us when it comes in the guise of love. But sometimes we don't even remember the many folks, the many loving acts that have made us who we are. People, imperfect as they are, can reach out at the right moments and express the hand and heart of God to us. Love is the only thing that can break through our walls of selfishness or fear or pride or ignorance. Nothing else can. Love focuses us on the needs and well-being of someone else, a world beyond our own.

A strong, loving, committed relationship provides protection against the world's distresses and threats. We share problems and pleasures. We become more aware of our virtues and vices. We divide the weight of our burdens. We're alert to life. Now love can penetrate us.

Because of love, we know we need each other, that we've got to talk to each other and try to understand. We're forced to communicate, to find some consensus.

Friendships become bonds deeper than family. Blood relatives become friends. Our children save us from toxic self-absorption.

A mother, a father, a family—that's where love is supposed to be done, discussed, created. That's community. That's social order. That's couples with a pledge. That's the skin of love, where we learn to do our real touching.

Joanne, only fifty-four, was dying of cancer. At the hospital, her family watched her rapid decline. But she refused to let go of life. Her overseas son hadn't arrived yet. Delay followed delay, and still she waited. Two hours after he patted her sallow cheeks and kissed her drooping eyes, she said her final "good-bye."

Love helps us hang on.

Love gives us a passion for connecting—just one more touch, before it's time to go. Love smooths the passage to the grave.

Several centuries ago John Woolman heard that Indians were on the warpath after suffering serious grievances. He got on his horse and rode out to meet the chief. He explained later what prompted him: "Love was the first motion, and thence a concern arose to spend some time with these Indians, that I might feel and understand their life, and the spirit they live in." The whole time he talked with them, he prayed for them silently, and at one point, out loud in English.

Later he overheard the Indian chief say to one of his warriors, "I always love to feel where words come from."[12]

Love has a spirit behind the words and deeds and gifts. Love gives us courage in the face of threats.

Love has empowered many to sacrifice careers and disappear into places like Africa or India or Brazil, to learn foreign languages and give years of life to tell of God's love. They dare to go, to do, to die.

One of the most potent forces of healing between the North and the South after the Civil War was the spirit of Abraham Lincoln. He refused a triumphal march into Richmond after the victory. When he arrived, on foot, he entered the room where Jefferson Davis had governed the Confederacy. For a long time he sat at the desk, his head bowed on his arms, and wept—for the fallen on both sides. The sight of the weeping president broke down barriers and healed wounds.[13]

Love gives us generous eyes and big hearts and far-reaching insight.

Jacob labored fourteen years for the hand of Rachel. Ruth left her home to care for her mother-in-law in a strange land. Jonathan risked his kingly father's wrath to warn David to flee.[14]

Love minimizes the strain of sacrifice, lightens the weight of burdens, steadies life's choices, gives us something and someone to go to bat for.

Charity is stirred by pictures. One heartwarming story arouses emotional investment in a faraway tragedy. Affections are the spring of action. Our affections keep us busy. We're motivated to act by love or hatred, by desire or hope, by fear or anger, by ambition or pride. If we had no affections, we'd be motionless, dead. We'd be involved in no activity.[15]

Affection moves us to cook a meal for a convalescent, to forgive the one who has done us wrong, to massage and tape sore feet, to give up the easy chair, to smile at the girl who doesn't smile back, to stay anyway, to make peace.

Love enables us to revive the romance in marriage, push on and press on and hang on with a friend, intercede for those who throw sharp stones.

"I can't love people in slices," said King Arthur in *Camelot*, "I take the good with the bad."

When we see faults through love, we see with spiritual eyes. We see people whole. Love covers a multitude of sins.[16]

Love places relationship above issues, above stresses, above conflicts, above projects. Love is a gift that makes us grateful, thankful people. When evil shatters us, love breaks through to transform us from bitter to better.

Love gives us a new name, makes us younger in winter, gives us a reason to laugh when nothing's funny. By it we survive, we thrive, we multiply. A person without love has no name, no stories, no light behind the eyes. The most tragic human sickness is loneliness. The saddest words that could be said of a child's party, a teen's graduation, anyone's funeral: Nobody came.

Someone who knows he or she is loved can be content with a piece of bread, while all the luxuries of the world cannot satisfy the craving of the lonely.[17]

Everything tastes better when it's shared. George Eliot once asked, "What do we live for, if it is not to make life less difficult for each other?"[18] But life overwhelms us. We're torn between loving and hiding, pride and loneliness.

Lost love is like a bomb blast—it leaves shards of shrapnel on mind and emotions. But a loving, intimate relationship is the ultimate healing arena. Love keeps us ecologically balanced: physically, psychologically, spiritually.

But how do we get the love?

Where We Find It

Love comes with practice, doing it over and over, realizing that with each person, each group, we need to learn a new language.

Love comes to us in moments of decision: there's something I can do now that I may never be able to do again. Bonding happens in one of those moments. Deeper attachments evolve in everyday choices—time spent together, loyalty tested, needs attended to.

We find love in touch. Skin communicates with skin: caressing a baby, hugging a child, high-fiving a teen, patting the arm of an adult. Touch means survival for premies and Alzheimer's victims. Our touch communicates universally understood love.

Touch teaches us the difference between "I" and "other," that there can be someone outside of ourselves.[19]

With the canopied shelter, the tough skin covering of love, plus commitment, over our relationships, we can do the rough business of truth telling, the tumbled business of trying to understand, the humble business of admitting we're wrong.

Love gives: food to the hungry, shelter to the homeless, help to the destitute, friendship to the lonely, comfort to the sad. In the story of the Good Samaritan, there's nothing romantic. It's a messy event, an impromptu nursing job on a mountain path, the stuff of quiet, obscure heroism. Mother Theresa and other smiling women minister to Calcutta's lowest caste, the dying homeless; they wash off layers of grime and wrap these poor people in soft sheets. They die anyway. Only the love lives.

We find love in speech: a different tongue, a heart language that at times only a loved one can understand. We love with words; words are powerful enough to either kill love or nurture it. We also find love in listening—to expectations and disappointments, to longings and sorting out mixed emotions, to humdrum details.

We find love in memories: the sounds, the smells, the scenes. We don't have to start all over again every time we meet. Memory helps us build, connect, and collect important events of the past, take them captive. We find love in the sounds of giggles and whispers, in the smells of movie popcorn and coffee breaks, in the sight of peeling wooden steps, all that's left of a place where people lived and loved. Memory can either feed the hate or cement the love.

We find it in family: in the genius of marriage, where love is taught and caught. The greatest need of children is "loving nurture that could produce fully functional adults with alive and responsive personal spirits."[20]

There are no perfect families. We're close, then we're irritated or cranky. We genuinely care, but at times we feel apathetic. But we don't have to be perfect if love's at the base. At its best, family is our support group, the handing down of love from one generation to the next.

Tears welled in Rivka Bromberg's eyes as her younger brother walked toward her. She thought he had died in a Nazi death camp. "Sister," Solomon Bromberg said simply, and the two embraced for the first time in sixty years. "I can't describe the feeling," he said, holding Rivka's hand. "I want to cry, but that wouldn't be enough."[21]

Love comes in letters, which can be "saved, savored, reread and treasured for hundreds of years"[22]: "My dear daughter," "Dear sweet friend," "Hey, meathead."

"How earnestly I long to hold to my fluttering heart the object of my warmest affections; the idea soothes me. I feast upon it with a pleasure known only to those whose hearts and hopes are one... [in] the absence of my dearest friend," wrote Abigail Adams to her husband, John, gone to war.[23]

Letters can simply perform a duty . . . or mingle souls.

We find love in forgiving—"we win by tenderness: we conquer by forgiveness."[24]

True love isn't blind. It sees everything—the faults, the irritations, the sins—and offers no excuses. Yet in time it reconciles and tries hard to kill the lingering resentments and every wish to humiliate, to hurt, to pay back. It's the reason Hallmark and Dayspring provide a line of "I'm sorry" cards.

We find love in watching the rain from the same window, listening to a storm from the same bed, grabbing a hand and not letting go. We show love in planning a special surprise.

I heard of a farmer who talked his wife into a spur-of-the-moment plane ride. While gliding over his field she gasped as she spotted the plowed message over a thirteen-acre plot of ground, "I love you." It was their tenth anniversary.

In 1990, Robertson McQuilken resigned as president of Columbia International University in South Carolina, to give full-time care to his wife, Muriel, stricken with Alzheimer's.

"It was only fair," McQuilken said. "She had cared for me for almost four decades with marvelous devotion; now it was my turn. If I took care of her for forty years, I would never be out of her debt."[25]

True love enjoys the best, forgives the worst.

Love is the face of one long-cherished. Only love can hold a withered, aged hand and feel a warm glow. Love kisses a cheek or a forehead and leaves a soul singing.

Love is not easily laid to rest. When distance, death, or change of heart rudely intrudes, leaving us empty and mourning, we need that desperate season of restless remorse to do our full measure of grieving and healing.

Love moderates "the violence of love of self."[26]

Love can be generated. The pursuit of love—giving it, receiving it—makes a wonder of any life. Love has a math all its own: the more we expend, the more it multiplies. Love can be regenerated.

For by Thy Love I Live and Love

> Love is an exotic; it is not a plant that will flourish naturally in human soil, it must be watered from above.[27]

It is impossible to love without first being loved. Love is a communicable trait.

We can trace the physiological imprint on our body systems from the flush of romantic tingles, the surges of the sex drive, but we can't x-ray love. Why does it exist? What would be the motivation? The purpose? The first example? Hormones and endorphins safely ensure the propagation of the species. What mix of chance particles produced love, or, for that matter, what mutants caused evil?

Scientists have discovered a mother gene, an inborn trigger that prompts female mice to care for their young. When this gene is missing, mice show no interest in their babies. This particular gene, called fosB, is a kind of regulatory switch that turns on other genes in response to outside cues, probably the sight and smell of baby mice.

Humans, too, have a fosB gene. While many believe genes, and genes alone, influence all human behavior, this is a sensitive point and is difficult to sort out. Learning, experience, and social conditions are also clearly important.[28]

Billy Sunday once said, "If the devils in hell ever turned pale it was the day mother's love flamed up for the first time in a woman's heart."[29] A mother's love is the closest human equivalent to God's.

God's cosmic generosity is poured into our world every day. His love is alive, bountiful, throbbing with creativity. He unties knotted things and ties up things dangling loose. His love holds all things together, sustains the universe. It's not a scarce resource or a rare commodity, but only the eyes of wonder recognize it.

Without God, there would be no love. None of us has ever known a moment devoid of the presence of God's love. But Jesus did. On the cross. And the moment was excruciating, unbearable: "My God, my God, why have You forsaken me?" He cried.

Those who claim they know love without God's help, without a whit of acknowledging Him, have never had their love tested in a completely godless world, yet. He's there for them, whether they know it or not. His rain falls, His sun shines on believer and nonbeliever alike, for now.

Those who know God through their spiritual senses, through the sense of wonder, say He is lovable, the most winsome, charismatic being in the universe. His love vibrates with electric intensity. But nobody could love God, unless He first loved us, because we could never know Him, unless He allowed Himself to be known. To receive an invitation of friendship with God is to be fully awakened, to come alive in the spirit, to know love's Alpha and Omega.

No one could be more justly loved than God, no one deserves our love more.[30]

The theologians tell us that God loves us for His own sake. He loves in us Himself—His virtues, His work, His gifts, His image.

The earthly life of Jesus is love's highest, richest, most vigorous expression. To study Him intently forces, at the least, the wonder of cold admiration or the burgeoning fire of worship. His death on the cross was love's most brilliant act.

Hell is a place where God showers no virtue, no help, no hope. He locks the dungeon and throws away the key to Himself. It's a place totally, completely deprived of love.

"Why do bad things happen?" we ask. The evil, the sorrows, the tragedies, the pall of death, love's greatest thief. We live in a day of the terrorist mentality—smash everything to make a better world, murder as many as you can to make a political statement. Destroy any relationship to preserve my own agenda. Random violence rules.

One explanation is that the enemy of our souls and of our God rails against love by stealing, killing, destroying. The real wonder is that good ever happens with such relentless, calculated assaults against our best intentions and highest hopes and deepest loves.

We should wonder, too, knowing the separation, the dividedness, the dueling nature within our own selves, why we're able to love at all. What prompts us to care anything about someone else? About a neighbor's misfortune? About a town's plight? About a country's honor? About concerns beyond our own?

God's love wraps us, enfolds us, embraces us, shelters us, surrounds us, like mother and father love. When given and received, it's a stamp on the soul, a seal on the spirit. But it takes spiritual power and insight to "grasp how wide and long and high and deep is the love of Christ," a love that surpasses knowledge.[31] His love is generous, magnanimous. Our concepts pale. They're too tame, too passive, too tepid. But once we glimpse even a snatch of this incredible love, we can't help wonder.

Why did He create the world and all the life that's in it? Was He lonely? Bored? In need of a challenge?

Why did He create Eve for Adam, knowing the risks? Why didn't He abandon us to our fate? Why does He continue as the patient Father, after all these years, after all we've done?

Why did He allow His Son to die for sinners, making the Lord of the universe "vulnerable to the possibility that they would snub him and turn away"?[32]

Until we understand the *divine* love mysteries, we can never say we've seen the entirety of love's wonders. His mercies are numberless. They begin fresh every morning, new every night. And we need them all.

Every sand that drops from the glass of time is but the tardy follower of a myriad of mercies.[33]

God's love is creative and never idle. He redeems order out of chaos, restores beauty out of ashes, revives peace out of strife. His love is at work in individuals, families, and nations. God's love in us remolds, recasts our desires. If I love God, I desire to do His will, to advance His kingdom. If I love my enemies, I actually desire their good.[34]

Though the Norwegians and Swedes are different, they have an unbreakable tie that binds them as one people. Why? When Norway wanted her freedom, Sweden granted it out of the Christian spirit of the ruling family in Sweden. That generosity in giving freedom without war or bitterness created a basic soundness that flavors all their relationships.[35]

Some of the best race relations in the world exist between New Zealanders and the Maori. These relationships were forged by the wise diplomacy of a Christian governor and a bishop. They made sound economic laws that protected the land belonging to the Maori, fostering mutual respect.

In the early days, when there was bitter fighting, the Maoris also showed generosity. They sent word: "The white man is hungry. He cannot fight well. So we are sending some food to the white man!" That was never forgotten.[36]

God's love is a security, like the blanket clutched by a small hand. His love is discipline, like a slap on the wrist. His is a lover's embrace, holding us tight, accepting us wholly. His love provides our needs, with a dash of fun, like a salad with a side of juicy hamburger. His love is healing like a wound packaged with its own dressing and salve. His love is the railing on a high bridge—it prevents us from going over the edge.

Everything God does, He does in love. But His love always comes with a companion: love and holiness . . . love and justice . . . love and power . . . love and mercy . . . love and knowledge and wisdom. His acts of love encompass all these attributes. They completely fulfill His perfection.

Our love, alone, can be unstable. We need the company of love and persistence, love and good temper, love and sacrifice, love and reverence, love and commitment, love and common sense. Love is a boat with a motor; it needs fuel and a rudder. Even then our love acts are incomplete, imperfect. Only when we connect to God's wisdom can we approximate love that works the best for everyone involved.

No human being is completely lovable. Some of what we are is wonderful. But some of our attitudes, habits, and mannerisms would be annoying to even a saint.

God's love is never fickle nor in need of growing and learning. His love is pure and all-knowing. He sees all needs and His plans simultaneously. Out of that vision, He acts.

Alice received her first sourdough starter from a friend. She was often teased about that wad of dough. Her family said she cared for it like a spoiled pet. She kept it healthy with a weekly maintenance of flour and liquid "feedings." In fifty-two years she claims to have adopted out hundreds of other starters to family and friends. It also made the lightest of pancakes and chewiest of breads. But it stayed its freshest when she used it or gave it away.

Love is a gift of God but a gift that requires ceaseless kneading, constant feeding, a timely schedule of giving away. Love is the wonder of a long, involved story. Love keeps going and going. Love lasts.

Exploring the Wonder

1. What would it be like to live in a world solely guided by the principle of love? Every race, every social class, every nation, every individual pledged to one thing: doing every act out of love for God and love for people. What would be the most major changes from the world as we know it now?

2. What is hardest for you—doing loving acts for people or feeling love for others? Give an example.

3. What is your most valuable possession?
   Under what circumstance could you perceive sacrificing that possession for
   • someone you love?
   • someone you barely know?
   • someone you hate?

4. Make a list for a child or a spouse or a friend of the things about him or her you wouldn't change for all the money in the world.

5. Share with someone the most incredible example of love that you have witnessed or experienced yourself.

6. What clues do we find in these verses for loving those who don't love us back? Why should we even bother?
Proverbs 24:17–18
Proverbs 25:21–22
Matthew 5:43–48
Luke 6:27–36
John 15:12
Romans 12:14, 20

7. Match the right verse answers below with the following questions:

1.___ What is love proof of?   a. Hosea 1:1–9; 3:1–5
2.___ What does love do for   b. John 3:30
    our deeds and   c. John 13:35
    accomplishments?   d. 1 Corinthians 13:3
3.___ What does love do for   e. 1 Corinthians 13:5
    our characters?   f. 1 Corinthians 13:7
4.___ What does it control?

5.___ What does it give up?
6.___ How much would we
      sacrifice for love?

8. Make this month your "love" month: read a section a day about love.
   1. Leviticus 19:11–18
   2. Psalm 103:8–18
   3. Lamentations 3:22–33
   4. Micah 6:8; Proverbs 19:22
   5. Matthew 5:43–48; 22:34–40
   6. John 13:34; 15:9–17
   7. Romans 12
   8. Romans 13:8–14
   9. Romans 14
   10. Galatians 5:13–26
   11. Ephesians 4
   12. Philippians 1:1–11
   13. Philippians 2
   14. Colossians 3:12–14
   15. 1 Corinthians 13
   16. 2 Timothy 1:16–18
   17. Philemon
   18. Hebrews 10:24–25
   19. Hebrews 13:1–2
   20. James 2
   21. 1 Peter 1:22–2:1
   22. 1 John 3:11–18

23. 1 John 4:7–19
24. Luke 7:36–50
25. 1 Samuel 20
26. Ruth 1:14–18
27. Psalm 145:8–21
28. Jeremiah 31:3–6
29. Psalm 23
30. Psalm 33:20–22
31. Ecclesiastes 3:1–8

Notes

1. Robert McCracken, "Commitment Unlimited," *Twenty Centuries of Great Preaching,* vol. 12 (Waco: Word, 1971), 89.
2. Song of Songs 8:6–7.
3. Adapted from "Pulpit Helps," *Austin Avenue Newsletter,* February 1996, 25.
4. James Thurber, in Joseph Stowell, "A Love Like That," *Today in the Word,* February 1995, 3.
5. Henry Drummond, "The Greatest Thing in the World," in *The Guideposts Treasury of Inspirational Classics* (Carmel, N. Y.: Guideposts Associates, 1974), 18.
6. Harold Sala, "Loving in Slices," *Guidelines for Living,* April 1996, 6.
7. Annie Dillard, *An American Childhood* (New York: Quality Paperback Book Club, 1987), 151.
8. Anastasia Toufexis, "The Right Chemistry," *Time,* 15 February 1993, 51.

9. Alan Bloom, "Relationships," in *The Closing of the American Mind* (New York: Simon & Schuster, 1987), 134.

10. Drummond, "The Greatest Thing," 25.

11. John of the Cross, "Rule of Life," in *You Set My Spirit Free,* arr. and paraph. David Hazard (Minneapolis: Bethany House, 1994), 64.

12. Rufus Jones, "The Two Loves—Agape and Eros," in *Twenty Centuries of Great Preaching,* 312.

13. E. Stanley Jones, "The Generous Eye," in *God's Treasury of Virtues* (Tulsa: Honor Books, 1995), 263.

14. See Genesis 29; Ruth 1; 1 Samuel 19–20.

15. Jonathan Edwards, "Religious Affection," quoted in Richard J. Foster and James Bryan Smith, eds., *Devotional Classics* (San Francisco: HarperCollins, HarperSan Francisco, 1993), 20.

16. James 5:20; 1 Peter 4:8.

17. Frances Roberts, "Love Endures," in *On the High Road of Surrender* (Palos Verde Estates, Cal.: King's Press, 1973), 91.

18. George Eliot, quoted in William J. Bennett, ed., *The Book of Virtues* (New York: Simon & Schuster, 1993), 182.

19. Diane Ackerman, "The Power of Touch," *Parade,* 25 March 1990, 5.

20. John Sandford and Paula Sandford, *Waking the Slumbering Spirit,* ed. and expanded Norm Bowman (Arlington, Tex.: Clear Stream, 1993), 8.

21. Dafna Linzer, "I Want to Cry, but That Wouldn't Be Enough," in *Lewiston (Idaho) Morning Tribune,* 24 July 1996, 2A.

22. Alexandra Stoddard, *Gift of a Letter* (New York: Avon Books, 1990), 9.

23. Abigail Adams, quoted in *Great Americans in Their Own Words* (New York: Mallard Press, 1990), 66.

24. F. W. Robertson, "The New Commandment of Love," in *Twenty Centuries of Great Preaching*, 388.

25. Robertson McQuilkin, "Muriel's Blessing," *Christian Reader*, July–August 1996, 37.

26. Jean-Jacques Rousseau, quoted in Bennett, *The Book of Virtues*, 107.

27. Charles H. Spurgeon, "June 11," in *Morning by Morning* (Westwood, N. J.: Barbour & Co., 1990), 125.

28. Wire Service Reports, Boston, "Scientists Discover Maternity Gene," *Lewiston (Idaho) Morning Tribune*, 27 June 1996, 2A.

29. Billy Sunday, "Motherhood," in *Twenty Centuries of Great Preaching*, 250–51.

30. Bernard of Clairvaux, "The Love of God," in *Devotional Classics*, 40.

31. Ephesians 3:18–19.

32. John R. W. Stott, *The Cross of Christ*, (Downers Grove, Ill.: InterVarsity Press, 1986), 216.

33. Spurgeon, "May 16," *Morning by Morning*, 105.

34. Horace Bushnell, "Christ Regenerates Even the Desires," *Twenty Centuries of Great Preaching*, 98.

35. E. Stanley Jones, "The Generous Eye," 262.

36. Ibid., 263.

ᔰ *Eight* ᔰ

NEVER A PANIC IN HEAVEN
The wonder of a big plan

Even when things seem to the contrary, I believe his universe and my life in it are unfolding as they should, and everything is on schedule.[1]

There are many ways to perceive this world:
- that what you see is all there is or all you need to know;
- that we're governed by chance, ruled by fate;
- that life's a barren, bleak, empty existence, each footprint leading nowhere, beside a tossed-up pile of driftwood, across a monotonous stretch of shifting sand;
- that if anything's going to happen, we'd better get busy and make it happen;
- that life is a math game, "a series of problems waiting to be paired up with their matching solutions, like socks";[2]
- that life is all in the mind, that happy or gloomy thoughts make the day a delight or an ordeal;
- that life's ruled by fearsome forces, evil spirits, and demons who can attack at any moment;
- that there's a loving, powerful being who oversees all of life's events, a God not limited by time and space, birth and death, who has a benevolent plan and the power to see it through, and everything's on schedule.

Honest reasoning has to concede that there could be a celestial plan.

For instance, why is it we want to know what's behind it all—not only the hows but the whys? Why should we care? No other creature does.

We, ourselves, are great planners. Where did that come from in a chancy, random world?

Stories make sense to us only if they have a beginning, a middle, and an end.

> The sun can shine daily, ripening the corn, and no explanation seems to be called for. A single flash of lightning kills a man and we feel immediately that someone "upstairs" ought to explain himself.[3]

If there were no sovereign planner, no one greater than the ambitious rulers and nations, no one stronger than the torrents and tempests of nature, no one more savvy or saintly than the plotters of evil, to whom could we appeal?

To produce anything of value requires a plan—blueprints for houses, engineering for freeways, patterns for clothes. We'd never leave any human endeavor to random selection, letting it just happen no matter how long we had to wait. Not even if we wanted a simple toolshed or a sack dress. If mindless swirling of primeval vapors and bubbling waters eventually became human life, why wouldn't randomness be the way of our nature?

There's an observable underlying order to most events. Who thought it up? There's a flow to the unfolding of history. Who oversees it?

The eyes of reason begin to see the faint outlines of His blueprint, the semblance of His design, by recording the sightings and thinking it all through. But where's the hard evidence?

Isn't it also plain that God's will is not primarily being done by humans?

Isn't God's earth, at least in part, lying in ruins?

Aren't God's plans largely ignored?

Isn't there plenty of pain and violence, mystery and confusion, atrocity and dying here on terra firma? How do His plans fit with all that?

Or has He given up trying?

Everything's on schedule. And that implies some kind of arrangement, some steps in mind for attaining an object, for pursuing a goal.

Everything's on schedule. And that presupposes exacting detail, a well-formed scheme.

Everything's on schedule. And that gives the strong impression of someone in control. We recognize this principle in human endeavors.

For a city to sponsor the Olympic Games is an incredible undertaking requiring years of preparation: arenas, stadiums, and construction or renovation of other facilities; accommodations for the hundreds of languages and nationalities; development of plans to manage traffic; institution of security checks, the scheduling of events, the management of ticket sales; the training of contestants; planning the spectacular opening and closing ceremonies; arranging for media coverage; assuring sufficient housing and meals; passing the flame across the continents; fundraising; organizing and training tens of thousands of volunteers; finding judges, officials, and musicians—can you imagine administrating a two-week party with a guest list of several million people?

Yet this extensive planning pales alongside a universal plan with a purpose. Does one exist?

If so, there has got to be one phenomenal planner at the head. We awaken to the sense of wonder when we realize there is a higher order above us, a preeminent being over us, who has both the power and the right to rule. He's head of the organizing committee. He's capstone and cornerstone, the vanguard and the rear guard of a mighty plan.

A Plan for the Universe and for Planet Earth

> Long ago all the galaxies and this very planet were brought into existence out of watery chaos by God's word. . . . The current galaxies and earth are fuel for the final fire.[4]

Even if we consider any part of the examinable physical world as crudely fashioned or so familiar as to be considered ordinary, we know we had nothing to do with its existence and we couldn't conjure up an *original* seed of it in our laboratories, no matter how long we tried. The best we can do is make copies. Or isolate the producers. We can't create life from nonlife, from nothing. Our illusions of power make us arrogant. We think we've solved the riddles of the universe when we isolate a fragment of it with our instruments and tubes. And label it.

But if we could take the place of God, would we trust any human being in this world with such an ability? Would that make us feel safe, well cared for, full of hope for the future? Doesn't even the concept of genetic engineering send an uneasy chill down our spines?

After that consideration, don't we feel a corporate sigh of relief to read

> The LORD has established his throne in heaven, and his kingdom rules over all. . . . according to the plan of him who works out everything in conformity with the purpose of his will.[5]

A thinking, caring, rational being maintains the controlling interest over the entire expanse of the universe and is overseeing the minutest aspects and details, including the fertile grounds of rich, rustling grass and the parched, cindered bleakness of dust bowls. That's one interpretation.

There's another: that we're rudely thrust into "a mindless universe cyclically doing its thing to no end."[6] Or that we're merely "organisms [that] were cobbled together layer upon layer by a tireless tinkerer."[7] If that's true, then we're the best there is.

On the other hand, it seems that our universe is largely dead. Looking into the heavens, it seems that there's an unfinished project of celestial proportions. Perhaps an aborted plan? Or something temporarily stalled? Because of events on planet earth?

Incredible Interdependency

At least one thinking man has observed, "In the early expansion of the universe there has to be a close balance between the expansive energy [driving things apart] and the force of gravity [pulling things together]. If expansion dominated then matter would fly apart too rapidly for condensation into galaxies and stars to take place. Nothing interesting could happen in so thinly spread a world."[8]

For the simplest, most basic act of life to occur, so many processes and ingredients need to coexist and happen simultaneously. Think about it. Seriously. How could any living thing begin and evolve without the perfect resources and without a plan? And how can there be a plan without a mind? And from where and how did the first thought come? That's the deepest enigma. Especially if there is no God.

Is Providence the care of a Supreme Being over the universe, who also has the formulas and procedures to create?

Or is it merely the capital of Rhode Island?

A Plan for Nations and for Humanity

From one man he made every nation of men, that they should inhabit the whole earth; and he determined the times set for them and the exact places where they should live. God did this so that men would seek him and perhaps reach out for him and find him, though he is not far from each one of us.[9]

Every group has a unique story.

Sumer, the first true civilization, produced the first creative writing, the *Epic of Gilgamesh*.

Mesopotamia, between the Tigris and Euphrates rivers, produced the first farms and provided for experimenting of artisans and builders while allowing for others to be leaders and warriors.

The Akkadians, the Amorites, the Mayans, the Incas, the empires, the monarchies, the dynasties, the inquisitions and crusades, the Marco Polos and Pizzaros: their histories are the birth and death of peoples.

We comprehend the impact of nations—with all their hopes, their rising stars, their dreams of glory, their unified pride, the sense of destiny through domain—if only through empty ruins. We often have to sift through rich sediments to prove our past, to know where we came from. All that's left for some are pieces of columns, fragments of pottery. Human kingdoms spill their broken jewels on the sands of time.

The history of humankind is incredible, no matter which line of philosophies or families or nations you trace. The complex harmonies, the rhythmic interplays. The interweaving of ancient tales. The tugs at the deepest needs of the human spirit. The ever-present warnings of disaster combine with friendly challenges to play, to dance, to cooperate with a fine-tuned mapping of the nations, charting of communities, diagramming of cities, and assignments for individual citizens. In history we catch a glimpse of the biography of God.

Sometimes we have to witness the whole flow to understand the full scale of the drama, the repeated actions and reactions, to know what God has done and will do again. Looking at the past is safe. It can't hurt us. It's done and gone. But we can draw insight and courage from a bigger picture for the present and future.

Israel got a special, personal covenant, a contract issued on Mount Sinai through Moses. God spoke through the prophets to keep explaining His wishes, to tell who He is, to express His love. All God wanted was trust and obedience so He could bless Israel and, through them, bless the nations of the world. So they'd recognize His Son when He sent Him.

> All the ends of the earth
>> will remember and turn to the LORD,
> and all the families of the nations
>> will bow down before him,
> for dominion belongs to the LORD
>> and he rules over the nations.[10]

Every nation established was conceived for a purpose, to complete its part of the divine plan. In this busy, rushing world, God always assumes an active role in the lives of individuals, families, cities, nations, and the universe.

A nation's lot often pivots on the actions of an individual. Joan of Arc led France to victory by encouraging lethargic soldiers in a number of battles during the latter part of the Hundred Years' War. She claimed France had a holy mission to fulfill. She contributed a female soul to the idea of heroism.[11]

The first Puritan and Indian harvest dinner . . . the Declaration of Independence . . . our first president's birthday. We have our way of designating important historical moments. God has His.

The year A.D. 40 marked the founding of the city of London, the birth of a future historian named Plutarch, and the worldwide spread of Christianity through the missionary journeys of Paul. God was intensely busy with all these events, each with a different purpose.

In spite of the misery and confusion that seems to prevail on our earthly scene today, everything is under the watchful eye of an infinitely wise God. Nothing thrown at us on this earth lasts forever. Nothing's wasted. He can use the worst and the most mediocre for good. Everyone has a choice—to do good, to go God's way, or to follow the violence of human ambition. People are responsible for their decisions. But God still presides over the destiny of Earth and its nations. And everything's headed for a good and righteous end. Because it's appointed that way.

And the end is getting closer.

This statement, spoken in the early 1800s, is still true today: "A dark and tremendous uncertainty hangs over the future history of the world. Events succeed each other with a rapidity that absolutely benumbs the faculties and annihilates the sensation of wonder. As much happens in the space of a single year, as would formerly have been enough to signalize a whole century."[12]

The character of God is revealed as much by what He does not do as in what He does. His patience displayed generation after generation. His anger restrained against blatant blasphemers. Rarely overriding freedom of will and choice. He shepherds the world with wisdom and tenderness. He rules by the power of love and the energy of goodness. He's no wimp. He's a wonder!

A Plan for Cities

When people are awakened by a call or nudge to pray for their city, the city gates open and the King rides in. We pray most intelligently by keeping two truths in tension at all times: Our cities have terrible problems. Also, our cities have terrific potential for accomplishing good for their citizens and for the world beyond.

> Seek the peace and prosperity of the city to which I have carried you into exile. Pray to the LORD for it, because if it prospers, you too will prosper.[13]

A nation is made up of a geographical and political alliance among its major cities. A nation is a sum of its cities. The cities are the mind and heart of the nation.[14] And they tug at the mind and heart of God. The human story begins in a garden and ends in a magnificent city.

John Dawson relates, "When I first arrived in Los Angeles, I felt engulfed by the vastness of the city. I felt small and irrelevant. How could anyone have an impact on a city so big, so impersonal and so diverse? . . . Only prayer changed my perspective. I began to have the mind of Christ, the attitude and perspective of Jesus. I actually wept over my city.

Now I feel God's compassion for the people of the city. I love my city. And I've seen it change—really change for the better."[15]

Cities are meant to be a "a place of shelter, a place of communion and a place of personal liberation as its citizens practice a division of labor according to their own unique gifts."[16]

If we have no vision, no idea of purpose for ourselves and our cities beyond our self-centered interests, obviously we can do no great work, accomplish no greater end.

New York City was originally the gateway of hope to the land of liberty. Now it's the hub of trade and center for world leadership. It embodies the dreams of wealth and power—it also crawls with crime and corruption.

Amsterdam has a centuries-old tradition of hospitality and tolerance; it's known as a city of refuge. Now it's also known for tolerating open drug sales and legal prostitution, a perversion of its original gift.

Could we ever imagine Hollywood as *Holy*wood? If it had enough intercessors, we could. Wicked Nineveh changed overnight in response to the preaching of the reluctant prophet Jonah. Because he finally responded to God's heart, to God's plan. And the timing was right.

Toronto, Ontario, an important international trading center, has a city hall that was constructed in 1965. It was designed by Finnish architect Viljo Revell after he won an international competition. The domed building is surrounded by high-rise office buildings, an enclosure of half circles that symbolize the arms of God around the city.

Lynne Juarez had a vision of building a "field of dreams" in downtown San Francisco. Where once there was a bleak playground that resembled a giant parking lot, now there is an inviting play area and gardens that nourish not only hummingbirds and butterflies, but inner-city kids and their neighbors. It's a natural environment, an oasis, which lives and breathes wonder.[17]

God longs to circle His arms around every city. If only we'd let Him. God is not a tyrannical enforcer. He's a Father.

In Wiener Neustadt, Austria, the congregation of Ichthys Church asked God to show them what was blocking spiritual awakening in their city. Through the library they studied the city's historically treacherous dealings with Jewish citizens over the centuries, up to 1938, when the twelve-hundred-member lively Jewish community fled the Nazi *Anschluss* to England, the Americas, and Palestine.

Convicted, the church confessed to God the sin of the city. Then they determined to do more. They located about sixty-five of Wiener Neustadt's former Jewish citizens and invited them to return for an all-expense-paid weeklong visit. The community asked these Jews for forgiveness, then feted them with a round of celebrations. Many wounds were healed.

"In the spiritual realm, an evil chapter has come to an end," said the pastor, "The power of God is starting a new era of history."[18]

Jerusalem—"Pray for the peace of Jerusalem" is the constant prayer command for the one essential city on this earth.

Jerusalem—the ground where King David, King Solomon, and Jesus walked. The city of tremendous promise and prophecy. The city of the most enormous perplexity when we don't understand the entirety of God's purpose and plan. And even when we do.

Jerusalem—the religious center of the earth—the pilgrimage for Jews, for Muslims, for Christians. Disasters should have long ago paralyzed her. She should be in ruin, as many times as she's been nearly and completely destroyed.

Jerusalem—no place on earth is more sacred, more loved, more rich in history, more turbulent. It's the world's most intriguing city.

When God's plan for earth is complete, He will create a new earth and a new Jerusalem.

The entire world may be on a collision course, but Jerusalem's destiny is secure, even when she's surrounded by enemies. It's part of God's wondrous plan.

A Plan for Individuals

Unless we're shouted awake, *zing,* the whole show shoots right past us and we never see a thing. It's so huge, so expansive, it's hard to conceive unless you've read the ancient texts and are watching for the signs. You have to study the wide spread of history from God's point of view. Even then you may miss it, until it touches down in some vital place in your own life.

At last count there were six billion people on our planet, all different, all precious in His sight. It's hard to comprehend the idea that God cares equally for each one. We don't really believe it until we experience it in some personal way. Then we marvel at the plan that He forms and watches over and carries to completion—the plan that makes allowances for our blunders, our blindness, our spiritual sluggishness. God achieves His will in us, through us, and in spite of us.

We know we've seen a part of the plan when the faintest cry is heard in heaven, when our prayers have been wondrously answered.

Monica, the mother of Augustine, was one of the most prayerful mothers in history. She spent her life praying earnestly for her wayward son. His life dramatically changed and he became a great man, fully awakened to the plan of God.[19]

We know we're participating in the plan when we're given sudden insight into a problem or given a wise plan of action.

The Bible tells of the "men of Issachar, who understood the times and knew what Israel should do."[20]

We know we've been a part of the plan when we've enjoyed an act of service as much and even more than the person we helped.

Dr. Paul Brand says, "I close my eyes and reflect on my life, flashing back through my memories to recall rare moments of intense pleasure and fulfillment. To my surprise, my mind passes by recollections of great meals, thrilling vacations, or awards ceremonies. Instead, it settles on instances when I have been able to work closely with a team and our work has allowed us to serve another human being."[21]

We know we've seen a part of the plan when events hint at who we are and what we were created to do, when our characters and gifts are being polished.

We know we've seen a part of the plan when we look back at our lives and discover that the crazy, dark times had a purpose. For Joseph, his call from the pit to the palace included a long stint in prison.

We know we've seen a part of the plan when we're in the right place, at the right time, for the benefit of many people. When our creativity or skills are especially suited for a task that meets a great need. When we've been set into a privileged position beforehand: Joseph in the pharoah's palace before the years of famine; Esther becoming a queen before the proposed slaughter of her people.

A friend, Joan, explains: "I had a feeling all my life that I was being prepared for something. When there was a crisis in my city, I knew it was my mission to pray and to organize supporters. Because I knew I was part of a plan, I had the determination to keep going, even when we faced ruthless opposition."

We know we've seen a part of the plan anytime things come beautifully together when they seemed to be falling apart; anytime a moment seems anticipated, expected, the details arranged by someone in the know, the outcome guided by many folks and events. Caesar crossing the Rubicon. Washington crossing the Delaware. Luther tacking his thesis on a door. Paul Revere taking a ride.

We know we've seen a part of the plan when we can see detours and providence, coincidence and benevolence, through a maze of twisted sin, so that some lost and errant one can make it back in.

We know we've seen a part of the plan whenever some evil deed has in some way been transformed to good, such as the unjust death of a holy Jesus becoming the means to an offer of salvation and eternal life for an entire sinful world.

Our best view of God's plan is in retrospect; then we can recognize the chain of events, the patterns, the turning points. We're the only creature with an appreciation for and awareness of its own past. God's plan is read by sensitive eyes, counseled by the years, educated by wonder.

But our tasks within that plan, like love, need daily attention and tending.

> When God planted a garden He set a man over it and set the man under Himself. To liberate that splendour, to let it become fully what it is trying to be, to have tall trees instead of scrubby tangles, and sweet apples instead of crabs, is part of our purpose.[22]

And our tasks can be done with the Big Plan in mind. As the worker on his job explained, "I'm not just building a stone wall, I'm helping to build a cathedral."

But the knowledge of this plan doesn't come without daily seeking and without willing assent. We pray, we study, we listen, we learn to love God. We carry out the duty of the present moment.

In the ancient days, when a squire was to be knighted he spent the whole preceding night in some cathedral face-to-face, alone, with God. From that holy presence he rode out to his adventures and his high endeavors.[23]

Most of our anxiety, our fretting and fussing, is due to ambiguity, not knowing what in the world is going on. So we can spend too much effort worrying about the plan. We try to figure how every circumstance and detail fits in, when all we need do is to fix our minds on Him.

> Our minds get into Lincoln Logs of logic: How
> does this fit together? How does this flow into that?
> We get so literal. But when God fills us with His joy,
> our hearts burst.[19]

It's a wonder that we ever were created—with all the risk and trouble, with the puny return for God's considerable investment. Doesn't every sin, every wrecked reputation, every atrocity, have at its core the selfish corruption of some gift that could have greatly benefited others?

It's a wonder we *still* exist, with our propensity for destroying one another, with our self-centered tenacity, with our habit of running from God.

But that would be assuming not more love from Him, but less.

And that doesn't take into consideration His glorious purpose. I can mess up my life but not His overriding plan. No arrogant human strength, power, or privilege can prevail against the rule of God.[25]

Though heinous plots devise the worst destruction known to humankind, they can't derail the divine design.

But why is it taking so long?

If the end is heaven, why dillydally around, century after century?

So that all may be gathered in.

So that one more soul may be saved.

The Finger of God

> *Why should God enter*
> *time, space,*
> *and created flesh*
> *to whisper His secrets*
> *to deaf-mutes?*

The Bible says that God does very little on this earth without telling one of His people about it.[26] Most of that's already been revealed. The plans of God are already there in the ancient writings. But some, like the apostle John, were given more information than they were permitted to tell. We don't know everything. Even what we've been told, we don't always understand.

Jesus explained to His disciples on at least three occasions that He was going to be killed. Then He would be raised to life on the third day. They never did get it. They were as surprised as anyone when this actually happened.

The plan is for people.

The plan is a work of redemption: restoring and redeeming a creative work that's been desecrated, vandalized. It's a search for what was lost. It's working to put things right—in a world gone wrong—in His time, His way. It's the procedure for pulling us away from sin and into humility before Him. It's meant to bring us safely home through the toils, snares, and rigors of this earthly pilgrimage. It's meant to produce what Dante called the "gradual shedding of error." It's God's campaign through history to get the better of human disobedience.[27]

God created not as a whim or a hobby but with a definite, eternal purpose . . . a purpose imbedded in goodness and wisdom, a purpose He's powerful enough to accomplish. He allowed the disorder to fall where it would, like pick-up sticks in the hands of a child. Out of it, He's creating a new order. And here and there we discover mighty monuments and secret signs that there's still a plan.

People are part of His plan.

He called Abraham to produce a son. Abraham got impatient and produced two sons. The sons produced families. Out of the families came nations. From one nation came the Messiah, God's Son. Jesus lived for us, died for us, was resurrected for us. That was the beginning of a new creation, a new people, a community of Jesus, the church, a major implement of His plan.

Angels are part of His plan.

Archangel Michael is the prime minister in God's administration of the universe. He's identified as the prince of the nation of Israel, fighting spiritual warfare on its behalf.[28]

There are millions of other angels who minister to people who are part of the plan.[29] We are the object of their special concern. There are times they encourage us, sustain us, lift our flagging spirits, and completely reverse hopeless situations.

We are always in the presence of God. We are always, too, in the presence of His angels. And we are a constant wonder to them.

> One day our eyes will be unscaled to see and know the full extent of the attention angels have given us.[30]

Lucifer, known as Satan, was an archangel who turned against God. He led an angelic rebellion. This is a deep mystery. We're often caught in the middle of that ongoing celestial battle, which is also part of the plan.[31]

The plan in one word: Jesus.

Jesus interjected the divine into human history. In His life we see the face of God. In His death we see the heart of God. His was the most prophesied, most predetermined life and death in the universe.

A brilliant stroke of genius: Through the cross of Jesus, God keeps every promise, follows through on every judgment, punishes sin with the death it deserves, steals Satan's thunder forever, stays completely true to Himself, defeats His enemies and ours, and gives His pitiful creatures a chance at life. He provides the ultimate weapon over evil—the ultimate, potent force that shakes the foundations of the

NEVER A PANIC IN HEAVEN

universe: holy innocence voluntarily dying in a guilty one's place.

Our prayers further the plan.

Praying in the light of God's Big Plan makes us conscious of the needs of other people and of cities and nations. We become aware of much more that God's doing around us. The highest prayer is asking that His kingdom come, His will be done, trusting in His goodness and perfect plan for any person or situation.

Many times the answers to our prayers, the enactment of miracles, has to do with whether or not they coincide with God's greater plan, His higher purpose.

A Canaanite woman (a foreigner) cried out to Jesus, "Lord, Son of David, have mercy on me! My daughter is suffering terribly from demon-possession."

Jesus ignored her. When He was pressed about it, He answered, "I was sent only to the lost sheep of Israel."

The woman persisted, and she so impressed Jesus with her faith and reasoning that He made an exception. And her daughter was healed.[32]

Everything God does is part of His dual vision. He sees twice. We cling to "the facts." He holds, with omnipotent firmness to what He calls "My plan." Part of the art of life is to get some of the double vision of God, to see the world from His angle.[33]

Everything He does has more than one purpose. Even His prophecies for the future are multilayered: a meaning for those who first hear it, a meaning for some event many years down the road. Also, an encouragement or mystery to solve for people caught in between.

Everything He says and does comes out of a unity of His total character. The plan isn't drawn just from His love, but from His love, His holiness, His wisdom, His justice, His mercy, and His righteous wrath, all at the same time. He never suspends one attribute to exercise another.[34] Many times evil provides the backdrop, the black curtain, that highlights His goodness. Otherwise we might not notice it, appreciate it, hunger with all our hearts for it.

There's the plan of the ages and the plan for our time.

There's the plan for our nation and the plan for my life.

There's the plan for my neighbor and the plan for the stranger.

There's a rhythmic flow in the plan for all humankind.

But only wonder-filled eyes will see it.

Exploring the Wonder

1. Try drawing a timeline of your life, beginning at birth. Graph the ups and downs. Star the highlights and darken the low times.

2. What do you know for certain, beyond all shadow of doubt
   • about yourself?

• about life on earth?

• about God?

• about God's plans?

3. Do you find God's plan a comfort or a consternation? Explain.

4. Name at least one purpose for the phenomenon of pain.

5. What is the most persistent question you have to ask of God?

6. Looking back on your life, does it seem to be a random assortment of events, or do you see a pattern emerging? Do you find it a good one or a bitter one?

7. What do you think is your country's main purpose in the world? Your city's purpose? Your purpose? Why are you here in this city?

8. When have you witnessed God at work? How did you know He was involved?

9. What Scripture verses give you the most comfort in times of perplexing trouble?

10. If there were no universal plan, no Supreme Being in charge, what would this mean for you personally? For humankind?

11. Can you think of an example in the Bible where God changed His plans? If so, who benefited?

12. Read Exodus 12; Deuteronomy 8:3; Psalm 1:1–3; 119:9, 11; Isaiah 40:8; John 15:7; 2 Corinthians 11:3; Ephesians 6:17; Hebrews 4:12; James 1:22. What has knowledge of the Bible done for you?

13. Read Genesis 6. Think through what it would be like to live in Noah's time. What if you were a member of Noah's family? What would be your response to God's directions?

14. Read Habakkuk. How did this prophet come to an understanding of God's great plan, and what was his response? What is your own response?

15. What is the biggest problem you face today? What could possibly be a purpose in this situation that fits into God's plan for your life?

16. What has been the biggest catalyst in your experience to either annihilate or accelerate your sense of wonder?

Notes

1. Charlie W. Shedd, *Brush of an Angel's Wing* (Ann Arbor, Mich.: Servant, 1994), 9.
2. "Sinking Ships," *Partnership*, 41.

3. Harry Blamires, "Providence," in *On Christian Truth* (Ann Arbor, Mich.: Servant, 1983), 40.
4. 2 Peter 3, *The Message,* 587–88.
5. Psalm 103:19; Ephesians 1:11.
6. Ravi Zacharias, "The Romance of Enchantment," in *Can Man Live without God?* (Dallas: Word, 1994), 79.
7. Ibid., 81.
8. Ibid., 84.
9. Acts 17:26–27.
10. Psalm 22:27–28.
11. Edith Deen, "Joan of Arc—The Deborah of France, A.D. 1412–1431," in *Great Women of the Christian Faith* (Westwood, N. J.: Barbour & Co., 1959), 60.
12. Thomas Chalmers, "Fast-Day Discourse," in *Twenty Centuries of Great Preaching* (Waco: Word, 1971), 286.
13. Jeremiah 29:7.
14. Peder J. Zane, "Giving Kids Hope," *Parents,* June 1996, 176.
15. John Dawson, quoted in Zane, "Giving Kids Hope," 36–37.
16. Zane, "Giving Kids Hope," 39.
17. Sharon Mumper, "From Pogrom to Peacemaking," *Christianity Today,* 12 August 1996, 38–39.
18. Dawson, "A Call to the City," in *Taking Our Cities for God* (Lake Mary, Fla.: Creation House, 1989), 36.
19. Edith Deen, "Monica—Mother of Augustine," in *Great Women,* 21.
20. 1 Chronicles 12:32.
21. Paul Brand, M.D., and Philip Yancey, "Service," in

Fearfully and Wonderfully Made (Grand Rapids: Zondervan, 1980), 49.

22. C. S. Lewis, "Charity," in *The Four Loves* (New York: Harcourt Brace Jovanovich, 1960), 164–65.

23. Arthur J. Gossip, "The Clash of Age and Youth," in *Twenty Centuries of Great Preaching,* vol. 8, 249.

24. Joni Eareckson Tada, "Heaven Can't Wait," interviewed by Holly Halverson, *Virtue,* March–April 1996, 24.

25. Rebecca Manley Pippert, *A Heart Like His* (Wheaton, Ill.: Crossway , 1996), 235.

26. Amos 3:7.

27. Blamires, *On Christian Truth,* 81.

28. See Jude 9; Daniel 12:1; 10:21; Revelation 12:7–12.

29. Hebrews 1:14.

30. Billy Graham, *Angels* (Waco: Word, 1986) 64.

31. See Isaiah 14:12–14; Ezekiel 28:12–17; Matthew 25:41; Ephesians 6:12; 2:2; 2 Peter 2:4; Revelation 12:4–10.

32. Matthew 15:21–28.

33. William E. Sangster, "The Pledge of These Glorious Scars," in *Twenty Centuries of Great Preaching,* 352.

34. A. W. Tozer, "Knowing God in Justice, Love, and Holiness," *Christianity Today,* 18 January 1985, 36.

✎ Nine ✎

OF MOREL MUSHROOMS AND LOGGERHEAD TURTLES
The wonder of small things

Pay attention to the small things—
the kite flies because of its tail.
Hawaiian Proverb

*B*ill was depressed, at a dead end, in his business and social life. He attended to all the daily duties required of him,
but he was stiff on the outside and barren on the
inside. Nothing interested him anymore.

One day at a company-sponsored seminar, a motivational
speaker challenged him to think back to the happiest
moments in his childhood. His mind wandered back to two
events: the discovery of mushrooms suddenly sprouted all
over the backyard lawn, and the time he stumbled onto a
turtle hatching.

The only vacation he remembered his family taking in
his childhood days in Savannah, Georgia, was out on an
Atlantic coast island. His uncle, his mother's brother from
Charleston, had been invited too, and he coaxed Bill to
go with him on early morning scavengings. Every day
they'd cart back to the cabin where they were staying
treasures and stories from the beach. But the last morning
was the best of all.

They were searching around a high and dry secluded area of the beach when a sand mound about ten yards from them erupted with an explosion—of baby turtles. Out spilled hordes—more than a hundred—of crawling newborn loggerheads.

Bill's uncle quickly motioned to him to lie down and stay quiet. They watched in hushed amazement as the nest opened wider and wider. The tiny turtles scoured their expanse of sand on their flipperlike legs for some time. They seemed to be searching for something, or someone. There was no adult turtle in sight. Then they scampered in a straight line toward the horizon, into the water, and slowly disappeared under the soft, lapping waves.

Bill was a researcher, even back in those days. He learned that the egg-bearing mama turtle's nesting instincts drive her to slowly and methodically pull up out of the sea to dry land where she can make a depression for a body pit, then dig and scrape a vase-shaped hole with a narrow neck and widened base. Her eggs fall to the bottom of the nest but don't break because they're calcified, like bird eggs. She fills the cavity with about 150 golf-ball-sized eggs, then covers them with sand. Then, she crawls down the beach and back into the ocean. Fifty to fifty-five days later, the babies are born.

Bill kept thinking about that mama turtle, all her efforts that produced that unexpected bonanza of wonder for him and his uncle to witness.

Bill's other memory was of the mushrooms and the underground buttons that form, just waiting for warmth and moisture to sprout and grow overnight.

The thought occurred to him that he was not putting any effort into making his life more than it was. He wasn't investing daily—planting any eggs or burying any buttons, so to speak—not providing potential for future wondrous results.

Bill applied the small wonders of nature to his daily habits in that marvelous way that the creative gift can do for any of us. His life became an adventure as he thought of one small thing he secretly could do each day to make possible some explosive surprise of wonder for the people around him. His first reward came when a customer told one of Bill's coworkers about a financial windfall, the result of some private groundwork Bill had laid for him—and Bill didn't even get the credit, but he enjoyed tremendous satisfaction.

Most everybody is interested in the big things. We want to be part of great events, important purposes. We like to think about those things and talk about them. But the world's crammed with so many small things.

If we add up the components of a day or of a year, we find it's comprised of small attentions—kind looks and deeds—that make the heart swell, that stir our sour existence into health. We may suddenly realize, through the lens of reflection, that some small event became an important beginning or a major turning point. We want to do great acts, but time passes and it seems we did nothing of significance at all. But "life is made up of 'infinitesimals,' " the microscopic, the minuscule, the tiny.[1]

A life consists of days. The days are made up of minutes. A minute takes sixty full seconds. Any big task consists of a hundred small details to get there. Housekeeping chores attend any venture we undertake. If we can't blaze like a star, do we refuse to shine like a firefly? If we can't make waves like the ocean, are we content to contribute to the trickle of a creek?

How was the wall restored around Jerusalem in the days of Nehemiah? By each man, whether his house was an old palace or the rudest cabin, building the breach before his own door.

A Small Awakening

The awakened mind sees the big picture. The awakened soul responds in gratitude and amazement to small wonders.

A farmer welcomes a swarm of ladybugs to his fruit orchard. He estimates that one of them can consume about seven hundred aphids in three weeks.

A cow isn't the only critter that has two stomachs. Tiny creatures, like some ants, do too—one for its own food, the other to carry food to its colony.[2]

I know a little boy named Jason who tells me that his praying mantis is the best pet he's ever had. It kills flies, eats out of his hand, likes having its back stroked, and when he ties it to his bed at night, it attacks any scary things that get too close.

The color yellow brightens any scene. Our eyes are attracted to it like a magnet. Yellow makes its own light, its own inner glow. It's a cheerful color. It splashes in a riot of shades—light and pale, medium and deep, radiant and rich. Some yellows are almost white, others nearly orange. It ranges from opaque to transparent. We don't have to like wearing it to enjoy it. Our world's washed in light, a sea of yellows and golds.

The eyebrows shield our eyes. They catch perspiration. They filter small insects and impurities in the air. They provide liveliness to our expressions—the lift of surprise, the knitted frown. They emphasize our eyes, the most expressive feature of the face.[3]

Who was the first person to propose the idea of a contact lens for the eye? Here's a hint: He was an Italian painter, sculptor, architect, and engineer. His name? Leonardo da Vinci.[4]

We're surrounded by small miracles. And when we start noticing the little ones, we'll more easily believe in the bigger ones.

As Jose Ortega y Gasset said: "To be surprised, to wonder, is to begin to understand."[5]

Small things can become bridges to the soul of another human being.[6]

A teacher was concerned about a child in her kindergarten who was cold, unresponsive to anything that occurred in the classroom. She tried every trick she knew, but the girl remained unmoved. During a regular sharing time, the teacher happened to bring a large wooden stack doll from her personal collection. The girl stared at the doll with the rest of the class, but with no expression. The teacher began to unscrew the top off the doll. The girl ever so slightly frowned.

Underneath was another doll, a bit smaller. Everyone in the room gasped. The girl ever so barely leaned forward.

The teacher kept twisting the dolls, exposing smaller dolls. Finally, she came to one less than an inch high. She asked, "Do you think that's all? Are there anymore?"

The girl slowly got up and stood next to the seated teacher. The teacher carefully unwound the tiny figure. One last bit of a wooden doll appeared. The girl reached out her hand and gently touched it with the tip of her finger. That was the beginning of the teacher's breakthrough.

If we empty the pockets of a five-year-old boy, we're privy to his secret thought world—there may be some string, a burned-out fuse, a chip of rock, a bit of candy, pieces from a pine cone, perhaps a toy sheriff's badge.

Peaceful overtures—meaningful communication between foreigners, people of contrasting cultures—begin with exchange of small, thoughtful gifts. Some friends are traveling to the Ukraine in a few weeks. They've learned from past experience that their hosts are highly appreciative of little tokens—like soaps and commemorative pins, like colorful ties and tie tacks. They greatly treasure items like medicines and panty hose, razors and a pair of jeans.

The Barnabas Committee

On a campus where the students and faculty were afflicted with a case of gloom and doom and negativism, one student began to notice a struggling professor in need of encouragement. This inspired her to begin a Barnabas Committee, a handful of students who committed themselves to pray for and encourage this man and other people on staff at the college. "We decided to remain anonymous," she writes, "to avoid embarrassment and charges of seeking favoritism. But we also wanted to communicate our concern and love."

Their solution was to type notes of encouragement, sometimes in silly rhymes, with small attached gifts such as candy bars, apples, or animal crackers. By the end of the year the mood across the campus had changed. The message was out: "Encourage one another."[7]

One of the powers of encouraging, even in little ways, is that it does so much good and can spread so far. Our sin-tainted world seems to delight in *dis*couragement—putting others down, gossiping, criticizing, complaining. To be sincerely, truthfully positive toward others is a wonder in contrast.

The martyred German pastor Dietrich Bonhoeffer once wrote, "Do we really think there is a single person in this world who does not need either encouragement or admonition? Why then has God bestowed Christian brotherhood on us?"[8] It's one of the reasons God gave us the church.

We live like Christ by serving the needs of people: "smiling at someone who hasn't been smiled at for three days, taking a blanket downtown and giving it to someone. It could be anything."[9]

It could be a phone call or a poem.

A man who introduced himself as Brother Micah of Rockford, Illinois, called me to say how much a poem of mine had meant to him. He had shared it with many friends and it had cheered them too. He had no way of knowing how depressed I'd been that week, dampened in spirit about some failures. What a wonder that he would be prompted to call me clear across the country about such a small thing!

After Joseph Bayly's eldest son died, the young man's fiancée sent the Baylys a poem written by Dietrich Bonhoeffer. Titled "New Year, 1945," it had been written for Bonhoeffer's own fiancée just three months before he was executed at the age of thirty-nine by the Nazis.

Thirty years after Bonhoeffer's death and twelve years after the Bayly's son's death, the Baylys received a letter from a pastor they knew in Massachusetts. The pastor had been visiting a seriously ill woman in a Boston hospital. One day the pastor gave her a book written by Joseph Bayly, entitled *Heaven*. It brought her much comfort before she died.

The woman's name was Maria Von Wedemeyer-Weller, Bonhoeffer's former fiancée.

From Bonhoeffer to Maria, then from another grieving fiancée to grieving parents. From one of the parent's books to other hurting people. Then, through a friend of the Baylys, back to a dying Maria—across an ocean and across years, the ministry of encouragement had come full circle.[10]

The one learning to encourage pays attention. When we take notice of children's mud pies and caterpillars and dolls and butterflies, they learn that their ideas, interests, and emotions have value. When we take time to listen to a child's stories, we grow in understanding of his or her feelings.

This morning two men, headed for Siberia with a missionary singing group called King's Heirs, told the children at Vacation Bible School about their adventures. At the close, one of them challenged the kids: "Someday in heaven a boy or girl, a man or woman from Siberia is going to march up to you in the golden streets of heaven and hug you hard and say, 'Hello! Thank you so much! If it weren't for you, I wouldn't be here.'

"And you're going to have no clue as you think, 'What is this crazy person talking about? I've never been to Siberia!'

"And they'll answer, 'But you put your money in the offering plate in that little church down there on earth. And those people were able to go and buy Siberian Bibles with the money and bring them to my town. I read one in my own language. I believed that Jesus died for my sins. And now we are here in heaven. Together.' "

The man concluded, "And someday I'll be too old to travel to such places. And you'll have to go in my place. Then, I'll give you money to help you get there."

The little boy shared his lunch basket of two small fish and five loaves of bread with Jesus and the disciples and Jesus fed five thousand people with it.[11] We'll never run out of people to feed. Or children who want to give what they can.

So Many Wonders, So Little Time

There's wonder in finding a knot in a piece of wood, the spot where a branch once grew out of the tree, the hard lump from the point of emergence.

There's wonder in playing with and mixing the colors on an artist's palette: cobalt blue with titanium white, terre verte with lemon yellow, raw sienna with a touch of burnt umber.

There's wonder in making music together.

There's wonder in waiting for the morning mail.

There's wonder and healing in a hearty laugh.

There's wonder in movement—in the sky, on the rocks, a dart outside a window, any stir against a still background.

There's wonder in the smells of wood smoke—pine, birch, maple, or oak, a whiff of apple, cherry, or tamarack.

There's wonder in a safe, comfortable, uneventful commuter flight. There's wonder in a jet that's crowded with tight seating, no elbow- or legroom, babies and caged pets tucked everywhere, and there's no crying or yipping.

There's wonder in the presence of magnetite in the bodies of bees and bacteria and the brains of homing pigeons.

There's wonder in a tiny heart-shaped plant called duckweed, the world's smallest flowering vegetation, which floats on the surface of ponds, food for ducks and muskrats.

There's wonder in the racket that frogs make, like the sound of running your fingernail along a comb's teeth or like deep, low chuckles.

There's wonder in children singing a song they learned—when you want them to.

There's wonder in a small town church choir on key or in a moment of truth that leads to healing.

There's wonder on the first day of green tomatoes. There's wonder on the first day of vine-ripened beefsteak tomatoes.

There's wonder in remembering a verse when it's needed or in doing what you can, and it matters.

There's wonder in walking across a frozen lake, in children absorbed in quiet play when you need a nap, in feeling the heat of the sun after a cold chill.

There's wonder in a hello hug or a goodbye kiss.

There's wonder in snow swirling in the car's headlights or in an aimless drive through the country, where you find an old, abandoned World War II military radar installation.

There's wonder in fat-free potato chips that taste good or margarine that *lowers* your cholesterol.

There's wonder in every detail falling neatly into place, in someone asking your thoughts and you really can share them.

There's wonder in hundreds of boats on the lake with different colored sails or in finding an antique crack-eye marble.

There's wonder in a book with a startling, refreshing idea or in glints of firelight all over the room.

There's wonder in secretly planting flower bulbs in an empty lot or in discovering a zebra butterfly.

There's wonder in a coral-fire sun or in a creaking cedar swing or in a sprinkler that throws rainbows.

There's wonder in the beaches of Anchorage, full of glacier silt, like quicksand.

There's wonder in the scent of honeysuckles, in the drumming sound of a pheasant, in the creak of worn saddle leather.

There's wonder in company coming, a party mood, an autumn evening.

There's wonder in an automatic garage-door opener, a well-aimed slingshot, a coat hanger handy for a locked car door when you have no keys.

There's wonder in memorizing the Gettysburg Address, in ripples across the water, in sliced red cabbage in a salad.

There's wonder in one peacock feather fanned, streaked and topped with an eye of shiny indigo and aquamarine, yellow and orange, purple and black.

There's wonder in your skinny shadow when walking, in shadow patterns on the sides of buildings, in the interplay of light and shadow from a plane.

There's wonder in a dried white flower on green moss, redwood trees in the fog, a cat purring.

There's wonder in your mate bringing you Earl Grey tea, an extra pillow, and a massage.

There's wonder in someone remembering your name.

There's wonder in the service technician who says, "No problem. Will only take a minute." And it does.

There's wonder in a brimming basket of hot garlic bread, in a child using lint for mouse doll beds, in putting one foot in front of the other.

There's wonder in the mood of a smell, the memory of a sound, the mystery of a taste.

There's wonder in chimes at dusk, golden hushes, a misty melody.

There's wonder in entering a room and forgetting why, then reentering the room and remembering.

There's wonder in a lively conversation with someone who's nearly one hundred years old.

There's wonder in getting something better than you deserve or in an uncrowded day at Disneyland.

There's wonder in joining the party after sulking outside.

There's wonder in a father who's there for you, a mother who prays.

There's wonder in something lost, now found.

Who Despises the Day of Small Things?

Little things mean a lot.

I met Nan at a women's retreat. She was searching for her God-given tasks, her ministry in the Big Plan. I suggested to her a half-dozen opportunities that would test her abilities. Her response to each was the same, "That's just not what I'm looking for."

She wrote to me after the retreat with the same request. I sent her a number of other suggestions. No response came back, until one day she called.

"Janet," she squealed across the miles, "I've found the perfect opening. Will you be a reference for me?"

I prepared what recommendation I could. Several months later came the cryptic note: "They passed me over for someone with more practical experience."

Little things mean a lot.

> The tongue is a small part of the body, but it makes great boasts. Consider what a great forest is set on fire by a small spark.[12]

A simple word can make a cold shadow slip over our spirits.

Moral possibilities lurk in even small decisions and choices. A ham-and-cheese sandwich could be decadent if we're defying a doctor's strict orders—or if we stole the sandwich. A word can be careless or careful, vulgar or elegant, grim or welcome.

The heat, the cold, the blustery wind—one fierce, buzzing bee—can color our feelings for an event or for a day. A whisper is the slightest hint of a sound, the edge of a tone, but if we're not included we take great offense. One remark can sink into the heart and reap a lifetime of bitterness or inspire a noble deed.

Little things mean a lot.

I was hiking around a park and I heard, before I saw, a loud, boisterous gang crammed into and hanging out of a pickup. They careened around the corners of the narrow, winding road to the main fishing holes at the dock. Strolling past where they had been, I noticed a trail of strewn beer cans.

At the entrance of the park, another pickup zoomed past me. The back of it towered with some kind of belongings, tied down tight. A paper floated out and around and down on the road. From where I walked it looked like a blank page, torn in half, a very ordinary and unimportant piece of litter.

The pickup screeched to a halt. The driver, a man wearing a Las Vegas T-shirt, hustled out, picked up the paper and drove out of the park. What a contrast to the beer-can-throwing crew a moment before.

Little things mean a lot.

Nikos Kazantakis in his book *Zorba the Greek* tells of a time when he couldn't wait just a little. He discovered a cocoon in the bark of a tree, just as a butterfly was preparing to come out. He tried to watch and wait, but he got impatient.

He breathed on it to warm it. The case opened. "The butterfly started slowly crawling out and I shall never forget my horror when I saw how its wings were folded back and crumpled; the wretched butterfly tried with its whole trembling body to unfold them. . . . My breath had forced the butterfly to appear all crumpled before its time. It struggled desperately and a few seconds later died in the palm of my hand."[13]

Little things mean a lot.

"I handed her some gifts. Small things, silly things, fun things. But I had carefully thought about them and chosen them and wanted to show my love in this way. After all, it was her birthday. But she refused them. Said she wanted to forget this one. I felt she spurned my friendship, rejected me in one of the important ways I had of investing in the relationship. I took my gifts and went home."

Little things mean a lot.

The God of Small Things

How can someone so grand and majestic concern Himself with insignificant matters: the heartbeat of a sparrow, finding lost coins, planting mustard seeds?

"I tell you the truth, until heaven and earth disappear, not the smallest letter, not the least stroke of a pen, will by any means disappear from the Law until everything is accomplished."[14]

Isn't God too great to stoop to a worm's eye view of life?

> He makes me lie down in green pastures,
> he leads me beside quiet waters.[15]

Why do we find God in surprising places and, as Mother Teresa says, "in the most distressing disguises"? We see Him as a shepherd searching for one missing sheep. We see Him as a party-giver for one rascally sinner.

The world is a small thing to God. Can't He place the whole earth in the cup of His hands?

> God chose the foolish things of the world to shame the wise; God chose the weak things of the world to shame the strong . . . so that no one may boast before him.[16]

So Simple, So Essential

Even little acts are noticed in heaven. Feats that no one pays heed to here are applauded by angels. A cup of cold water given. A touch in the crowd. A poor woman dropping two bits of copper into an offering box.

> The man who had a pound given him and who used it well, must have been greatly surprised when he

learned that, as a reward of his fidelity, he was to be the ruler of ten cities.[17]

The God of the universe explains Himself through the commonplace.

Jesus claimed to be light, to be bread, to be the door. He is the door for the sheep.

A visit to Palestine illuminates the Bible's illustrations. The land and its people shed light on biblical images and stories. In the typical sheepfold there's a low wall made of mud and stones, but the opening has no door across it. Some tourists once asked a shepherd why. He replied, "I am the door."

The shepherd himself lies down at night at the opening. Nothing passes without touching him.[18]

Little words make a tremendous difference.

Jesus said, "I am *the* door,"[19] (RSV, emphasis added), not I am *a* door.

Jesus is the open door. No one can shut it. Jesus is the only door. No one can detour it.

> After all these years, the door is still open. God alone knows how soon the door will shut and no more sheep will enter the fold.[20]

A door has to be knocked on.
A door has to be opened.
A door has to be entered.
A door is the only way in, unless a window is pried, which is a break-in, an illegal entry.

A door provides protection.

A door provides a focal point to catch the attention of the master of the house.

An open door invites, appeals, entreats, entices, welcomes, woos.

Just before my husband graduated from seminary, he applied to serve as pastor at a certain California church. But the rules of the denomination seemed to make this impossible. So, one day he went up on a nearby mountaintop to pray about it. On his way home he drove by the church. He stopped his car, walked up to the locked sanctuary double doors, and knocked.

"Lord, here I am knocking," he said out loud. "Is there some way to let me in? I really want to serve you through this congregation."

Within two weeks a provision around the rule was discovered. He was called to pastor that church.

Malcolm Muggeridge commented, "All happenings, great and small, are parables whereby God speaks. The art of life is to get the message."[21]

God is not ashamed to do small things.

He does not always use angels or flashy miracles to further His plan. He usually assigns a human being. This helps form bonds, a community of cooperation.

> Being mutually dependent on one another, we are fused more completely into one family.[22]

What wonders can be wrought *without* miracles! We can see God's mighty works just as clearly through the situation comedy of the book of Esther—when He "allows everything to go on in the usual way, and gives mind and thought, ambition, and passion their full liberty, and yet achieves his purpose."[23] Or, through the purposed plagues against Pharaoh and the phenomenal deliverance of the Jews in their exodus out of Egypt.

When we're awakened to the wonder over our heads and under our feet wherever we go, we have good reason to constantly be thanking God for the simple, the wise, the good, the unadorned.

> *There is a gate that stands ajar,*
> *And through its portals gleaming,*
> *A radiance from the cross afar,*
> *The Savior's love revealing.*
> *Oh, depth of mercy! Can it be*
> *That gate was left ajar for me?*
> *For me . . . for me?*
> *Was left ajar for me?*[24]

There's wonder even in a door.

Exploring the Wonder

1. Just now, sit back, close your eyes, and try to imagine yourself in a place like this:

One summer afternoon a light wind waltzed across the lake, gliding along the glassy surface, dancing over the whitecapped surf, ruffling lavender lupines in the meadow. On nearby pines, the needles hummed softly in the breeze while the waves played up and down the sandy shore.[25]

Is this a place where you could relax or play, resting and refreshing your soul and spirit? Do you know a real place like this? If so, how long has it been since you've gone there?

2. One way to enable a simple wonder to last longer is to paint it on a canvas or to take a photo. Can you think of other ways to record wonders?

3. Just for fun, what do the following things have in common? Glaze, feather, scumble, crosshatch, a stick flat on its side. (Answer below.)

4. Have you ever viewed a small thing so near perfection that if just one item or unit were removed something would suffer because this thing is so expertly put together?

5. Self-pity cannot coexist with a thankful spirit—explain what this statement has to do with the wonder of small things.

6. Which of the little acts mentioned in these Scriptures would you like to start putting into daily practice?

Proverbs 3:3

Mark 6:31–32

Luke 10:5

Philippians 4:8

7. How does knowing that God is greatly interested in the little things and that He is author of the simple wonders affect your prayers?

8. Has God ever asked you to do a small task and you turned it down because you thought it wasn't important enough or big enough?

9. Read 1 Kings 19:11–13. How do you interpret what God is trying to say to Elijah?

10. Read Matthew 11:20–28 and Isaiah 30:15. With whom could you share the encouragement of these words right now?

(*Answer to Question 3: These are all different kinds of artist's strokes*)

Notes

1. F. W. Robertson, "The New Commandment of Love," *Twenty Centuries of Great Preaching,* (Waco: Word, 1971), 385.

2. Leonora Hornblow and Arthur Hornblow, *Insects Do the Strangest Things* (New York: Random House, 1968), 12.

3. Roberta Kramer, *A Book of Curiosities* (Middle Village, N.Y.: Jonathan David, 1990), 25–26.

4. Charles Panati, "Through the Medicine Chest," in *Extraordinary Origins of Everyday Things* (New York: Harper & Row, 1987), 268.

5. Jose Ortega y Gasset, quoted in *John Bartlett's Familiar Quotations* (Boston: Little, Brown, 1980), 784.

6. Tim Hansel, "Four Commandments of Contentment," in *When I Relax I Feel Guilty* (Elgin, Ill.: David C. Cook, 1979), 85.

7. Jeanne Doering, *The Power of Encouragement* (Chicago: Moody Press, 1982), 14–15.

8. Dietrich Bonhoeffer, *Life Together,* trans. John Doberstein (New York: Harper & Row, 1954), 106.

9. Lesa Caban, "The Right Touch," interviewed by Mona Gansberg Hodgson, *Virtue,* May–June 1995, 21.

10. Doering, *The Power of Encouragement,* 164–65.

11. Luke 9:10–17.

12. James 3:5.

13. Nikos Kazantakis, *Zorba the Greek* (New York: Ballantine Books, 1952), 138–39.

14. Matthew 5:18.

15. Psalm 23:2.

16. 1 Corinthians 1:27, 29.

17. Charles Jefferson, "The Importance of Little Things," in *Twenty Centuries of Great Preaching*, 61; see also Luke 16:10.

18. Walter Hughes, "Christ the Door," *Moody*, February 1986, 84.

19. John 10:7–10; see Acts 4:12.

20. Hughes, "Christ the Door," 84.

21. Malcom Muggeridge, quoted in Ken Gire, *Windows of the Soul* (Grand Rapids: Zondervan, 1996), 57.

22. Charles H. Spurgeon, "Encourage Him," in *God's Treasury of Virtues* (Tulsa: Honor Books, 1995), 233.

23. Spurgeon, "Providence," in *Twenty Centuries of Great Preaching*, 72.

24. Hughes, "Christ the Door," 84.

25. Review of *A Woman's Walk with God* by Sheila Cragg, *Good News Letter*, May–June 1996, 1.

☞ Ten ☜

MORNING IN OUR EYES
The wonder of awakenings

> The universe is a great organ with mighty pipes.
> Space, time, eternity are like the throats of this great
> organ, and man, a little creature, puts his fingers on
> the keys and wakes the universe to thunders of har-
> mony, stirring the whole creation to mightiest acclama-
> tions of praise.[1]

A missionary travels far into a remote Jamaican village
and finds awakened people who are playing that great organ
of the universe. "The people came in from the little paths all
around," he explains. "They sat in the little frame building
with no backs in the pews and one lightbulb hanging from
a cord in the center of the room. They had a little pump
organ up front that hardly worked. . . . But believe me, they
sang!"[2]

Awakening mentally means knowing and understanding.

Awakening emotionally means compassion and balance.

Awakening socially means developing sensitivity and
reaching out.

Awakening spiritually means worshiping and praising.
Awakening causes our spirits to soar with the angels and
our minds to marvel at the King.

Awakening means becoming more fully human through
loving nurture. The awakened are "fully functional adults
with alive and responsive personal spirits."[3]

Awakening slowly melts the ice-cold stoneness of the hardened heart.

Awakening happens when something or someone shakes us.

Awakening happens when we open our eyes, look around and assess, then get up and do.

Awakening happens when we knock our brains out trying to make something work, seek answers in all the wrong places, then come crawling to our heavenly Father asking, "Please help."

Awakening is a cooperative effort: our souls or spirits are nudged and we must budge. Forces work without and deep within "with the aid of the elements of daily life, its scenes and passions."[4] Our part is mostly a matter of paying attention and following instructions.

The healthiest awakening doesn't draw all the attention to ourselves but to the Lord who awakens us.

Awakening is a Rip Van Winkle affair, but it feels like a blast of cold air, a bucket of water splashed on the face, or being bumped out of bed.

It's looking into the jaws of death and seeing life for the first time. It's all joy breaking loose.

We have many ways of describing this phenomenon. And many avenues for experiencing it.

The Awakening Moment

My heart is stirred by a noble theme.[5]

The lowly dragonfly can see in every direction at once. But is he truly awake? Does he really know what he's seeing?

We can have our eyes open but fail to comprehend the sights with our souls and spirits.

Awakening happens when we look at something long enough and deeply enough that the scene grows transparent. We finally see through the window, not just see the reflection bouncing back at us.

Awakening can be abrupt and memorable. There's excitement—shouts, dancing, joyful singing, sparks flying everywhere. Suddenly, we have the right eyes. It's like experiencing a direct hit by lightning, and surviving.

Awakening is Jacob running from home and finding the stairway to heaven: "How awesome is this place! This is none other than the house of God." It's Moses before the burning bush "afraid to look at God." It's doubting Thomas discovering his God in the wounds of Jesus. It's Stephen about to be stoned: "I see heaven open and the Son of Man standing at the right hand of God."[6]

Or it can be quiet and almost imperceptible—a hushed rippling of a single heart that reaches out in soft cycles of secret and sweet reverberations. Awakening is the serious joy of bringing a touch of heaven to earth. It's a moment so close and still, we can hear God breathing.

It was a dark time in my life. I needed solitude, so I wandered away somewhere. I was camping near Mount Lassen. When I woke up I saw, framed in the tent door netting, the texture of white bark set against the bluest sky I'd ever seen. From that moment it seemed the land awakened all around me.

One day, when I was in the third or fourth grade, my class was bused downtown to hear the San Diego Symphony play a children's concert. One encounter with the *Nutcracker Suite* and I was hooked forever, . . . seduced and thrilled. . . . I got even more serious about serious music at thirteen.[7]

He made me laugh, a hearty kind of rip-roaring laugh, and it healed a hurting place deep inside me.

I remember running over the hills just at dawn one summer morning, and pausing to rest in the silent woods saw, through an arch of trees, the sun rise over river, hill, and wide green meadows as I never saw it before. Something born of the lovely hour, a happy mood, and the unfolding aspirations of a child's soul seemed to bring me very near to God, and in the hush of that morning hour I always felt that I 'got religion' as the phrase goes. A new and vital sense of His presence, tender and sustaining as a father's arms, came to me then, never to change through forty years of life's vicissitudes, but to grow stronger for the sharp discipline of poverty and pain, sorrow and success.[8]

It was at a time when I desperately wanted to personally experience the love of God—not just hear about it and read about it. I had even prayed about this with a speaker at the retreat I was attending. As I walked along the Atlantic shores of Virginia Beach, I noticed another woman and a teenage boy coming the other way. The woman made an abrupt ninety-degree turn, marched straight toward me, embraced me deeply, kissed my cheek, and whispered, 'I love you,' then continued on her way.[9]

One thing I do know. I was blind but now I see![10]

There was the fall that I dusted off my Bible, brushed up on the hymns I knew and began studying churches nearby with a keener eye. I had just heard a testimony by Charles Colson of Watergate fame. That led me to look up the blinding light passage of St. Paul on the road to Damascus. I was being reawakened by my own blinding light.

I saw myself as a sinner in the sight of a holy God. I knew I needed a Savior.

The more I pray, the more I understand the Lord and how He does things. . . . the more I feel God entering my soul to work in me and through me. And I am that much more alert to the brush of an angel's wing.[11]

I came to realize through a persistent, caring friend that a key to my wholeness as the person God created me to be was somehow connected with embracing and accepting the day of my birth, the day my mother rejected me. A simple thing, but definitely not easy. Every year the weeks surrounding my birthday I would experience a terrible depression and I wouldn't let anyone in, not even my friend. But she prayed and loved me and gently exhorted until I could release that day back to God.

I opened the Bible lying on a hotel table, and lighted on this memorable verse: 'Trust in the LORD, and do good; so shalt thou dwell in the land, and verily thou shalt be fed' [Ps. 37:3 KJV]. That was a turning point in life with me. Great spiritual illumination, unequalled in all my history . . . convinced [me] that I must make my own experience and determine my own destiny . . . and I was especially in mood to wait and watch for providential intimations.[12]

I was on my knees, deep in prayer, in awe of God's absolute holiness. It was a life-changing experience as I gained a completely new understanding of the holy God I believe in and worship.[13]

We read the stories clear through, from Genesis to Revelation. Here were all kinds of people who knew God. Sometimes they obeyed Him. Sometimes they disobeyed. But they knew Him, and we didn't.

Only God is capable of awakening our souls with a joy so sweet that it is, at the same time, a longing for him that is also painful and intense.[14]

We finally received our tax estimate from the accountant: we owed three times what we'd expected and didn't have the funds. After we pored over all the items in the prepared statement, I searched through the other pieces of mail.

That's strange, I thought, *a letter from my brother in the middle of the year.*

We rarely heard from him, except at Christmas. I turned the envelope over to tear it open. There was a "Jesus Is Lord" sticker on the flap. Inside he sketched the details of his spiritual awakening at age thirty-five and announced his upcoming baptism. The tax dilemma quickly faded. We celebrated instead.

The Awakening Process

All I have seen teaches me to trust the Creator for all I have not seen.

Ralph Waldo Emerson

Stories can awaken us. Characters can help us see ourselves, feel another's anguish, see through another's eyes. They can also provide unexpected instruction.

The narrator in *The Baronet's Song* explains the young boy Gibbie's philosophy of life: "There is a great deal more to be gotten out of things than is generally gotten out of them, whether the thing be a chapter of the Bible or a yellow turnip."[15]

Each moment we live we're either consciously staying awake or falling back to sleep.

Awakening is an enlargement—of the heart, the soul, or the spirit. It's the graced virtue that comes to the person who values aggressive control, making things happen, who prizes projects over people, contracts over compassion. It's nurturing harmony, listening in silence for a song.

When we awaken, we're children again, starting our wonder adventure, each day ready to receive any new thing God has waiting for us. George MacDonald remarks in his novel, *The Shepherd's Castle*, "We do not understand the next page of God's lesson book; we see only the one before us. Nor shall we be allowed to turn the leaf until we have learned its lesson."[16]

Awakening happens within a context, as part of a story. Though awakening may seem sudden, the sleeping spirit has been shaken for some time by events and persons and troubling rumbles within the soul. Changes are taking place and the sleeper is being aroused to respond because dangers are in the road ahead. Some work must be done. A vital choice must be made. Awakening can happen through any catalyst that causes us to come away changed. But we're still stuck somewhere in the middle of the story. The happy ending is out there, up ahead.

> Awakening is a process, a matter of degrees of sight.
> Just like working with a jigsaw puzzle, one moment
> we see only irregular shapes of green, the next
> moment we see grass; one moment we see only
> disconnected shards of blue, the next moment we
> see sky.[17]

We want the sharpness, the many dimensions of the original scene. But often we're seeing the photo of the scene or the painting from the photo of the scene or the photo of the painting of the scene or the magazine print of the photo of the painting of the scene. We have to be close to reality to see wonder. And then, the conditions must be right. The sun must be behind and the rain in front to produce a rainbow.

Awakening may begin on the outside with the actual organ of the eye gate. But the deeper awakening is within us, a soul happening, an inner spirit knowledge: loving an enemy, feeling another's pain, tasting that the Lord is good.

Awakening is a growing sense of the lack of knowledge, of something vital missing: A desire to know truth, a hunger for knowledge, a season of earnest study and seeking, a clearing of insight, an increasing ability to discern between falsehood and truth, a developing gratitude for the Giver of knowledge, a season of wrestling with choices.

The awakening mind needs a friend with whom to communicate, to discuss questions and evolving insights. An embryo faith often sounds like doubting. The awakened personality begins with the gift of relationship that understands such things, that sticks in there until breakthrough.

Every day we decide certain actions. Each day we choose to awake. Or not.

> Start each day with an "out loud" prayer in which you enthusiastically choose life, openness, relationships, love, vibrancy, and fun.[18]

In order to stay awake our minds must be nourished. To keep the process of awakening going to completion, we must at some point define what's happening to us and establish some deliberate habits.

Some signs, some stages, of awakening are
  • delight in daily pleasures
  • a hunger for more knowledge

- ability to recognize spiritual meanings behind natural occurrences.

The spirit stirs when we reach out to God through prayer, devotional study, active community with God's people, making private choices against sin, and interacting with the wholesome wonders of the world.

We can catch our own spirits or souls in the process of awakening. For instance, pay closer attention when you find tears in your eyes, especially unexpected tears. They are telling you something about the secret of who you are or where you've come from or where you should go next.[19]

The Awakening Tension

Like a tree, we are torn between two worlds, a part of us rooted in the soil, another part reaching for the sky. But because our roots can grasp soil more securely than our leaves can grasp sky, the soil seems more real . . . .

Yet something of the sky is taken into its pores, and something of the sun is taken into its cells.[20]

The awakened mind notices twice: both the lofty and the lowly. The awakened heart perceives and must confront opposite truths about itself: its total sinfulness and its capacity for great courage and faith.

We recognize the possibility of miracle, the super-natural, the unexpected—but we're also keenly aware of the potential for devastating evil. The awakened mind recognizes and accepts absolute truth and acknowledges the rights of human authority. It has a deep concern for hurting humanity, and active compassion for a few. It exercises creative imagination in some specific pursuit and maintains a general reverence for the sacred. The window opens between heaven and earth.

Awakened minds can feel like "pioneers in a strange and virgin country,"[21] because we bump hard against the secular mind wherever we go. In fact, a part of us is still strongly prone to mundane thinking, since that's the environment in which we're steeped.

Awakening, we learn that nothing is as it appears: no one is quite as evil or quite as good as we imagined. Just as every sparkling, rushing stream and waterfall is polluted in some way, every human being, however significant and loved, is permeated with some strain of poison.

Life's a mixture of elements: the uncanny and the ordinary, the awful and the holy. Sometimes the lines are blurred, mingling truth and lie, right and wrong, horror and wonder. But the difference is crucial. One gives us hope, enriches and fulfills life; the other degrades, destroys, violates the worth of a human being or the validity of God. The things of wonder provide the base for models, ideals, our highest aims and goals. Even with the increased awareness of evil in this world, we don't have to be paralyzed by its threats. We can overcome: the cross is our wonder monument.

Crashing cymbals

The newly awakened can be surprisingly noisy and bothersome to those around them. Now the awakened one wants everyone else to change too—everyone to wake up, even those who thought they were already wide awake. When the sleeping dead wake up, the results can be unsettling for a time.

And it's a painful thing to be misunderstood or misjudged. But it's like the character Malcolm said in *The Marquis' Secret,* "It's not more than God puts up with every hour of the day. But He's patient. So long as He knows He's in the right, He lets folks think what they like—till He has time to make them know better."[22]

In the same way we can be patient with those oblivious to wonder. They must sense their own need for awakening when someone cares enough to come alongside and point out the wonders, when someone has faith enough to pray them through the barriers.

Many awakenings

Awakening isn't a one-time event. Perhaps we can remember a first wakening, such as the moment of our earliest peek into the spiritual world, into the face of God our Father, into a world beyond our own. But waking up is only the beginning. Every day becomes another exploration, another discovery. We become like children again. Maturity should never be a frozen moment: "Ah, I am now all I should be, all I'll ever be. I shall remain as I am—forever." Maturity is understanding all we don't know and graciously opening our minds to new wonders.

As long as we're living, we cannot be entirely asleep. Nor is anyone completely, in every way awake.[23] We must always be looking and listening and learning, developing the disciplines of deepening awareness.

The proof of authentic awakening sparkles from a sincere inward attitude of gratefulness, thankfulness, and graciousness toward God's special gift of life. This attitude provides strength and energy for perseverance in good deeds.

Awakening also has a dark side. A very little thing can plunge us into the murky shadows of dread or repulsion instead of the pure innocence of delight: Looking at a pornographic magazine or an X-rated movie, attending a seance.

Sometimes we have to fight to feed our souls with better things. Just flipping channels or scanning newsstands or standing in grocery lines scars our minds with vivid, torrid pictures. Life's a concoction we have to sort out, sift through, and deliberately junk or save. Awakening is a journey "with many confusing branches in the road and much fog to obscure the vision."[24]

Awakening is neither a quick nor an easy process. We should not expect instant miracles of transformation from the one awakened, though it does happen. We all need lots of guidance along the way.

The Awakening Purpose

Often the best friend a man ever has is not comfort, but the stimulus and challenge of an antagonistic environment to awaken the resistance of his slumbering soul.[25]

When we aren't awake, we're careless, inattentive, inconsiderate, neglectful, oblivious, thoughtless—and life falls away from us like a knotless thread. Ingratitude is one of the greatest offenses against another person, against God.

Awakening does not put God at our beck and call. It makes *us* available to *Him*.

Awakening improves our prayer lives, widens our concerns, expands our visions, toughens our stance. Awakening causes us to stop accusing and prompts us to intercede instead.

Awakening makes church attendance a family appointment with God—to respond to His wonder, to be the first in line to be part of His Big Plan. We want to learn how to worship. A switch is turned on and we become pilgrims, hungering for other spiritually sensitive friends, seeking service in a sin-sick world, heading for the Celestial City.

> Community is a key element in the progress toward redemption and maturity. Why? Because at one level sin is also isolation or alienation.[26]

Awakening consoles us, fine-tunes and balances us. We learn to smile at life's fine ironies, admire its mysteries, and plug away at its necessities.

Awakening humbles our notion that we're at the center of the universe.

Awakening helps us know whom to thank.

And from my smitten heart with tears
Two wonders I confess—
The wonders of redeeming love
And my unworthiness.[27]

Waking up isn't worth much if we just lie there in bed and never get up and get busy. Eyes were intended to help us get from one place to another. God expects us to use our minds and hands to clean up some part of our world's mess.

We're awakened so we can deal with the ugly rooms inside our own souls and wash them with the tears of sorrow and forgiveness.

> Once the soul is opened and we know how to see beyond our *selves*, you could say, God will keep walking by.[28]

We're awakened so we can hear the cry of someone in trouble.

We're awakened so we can plant some seed of future wonder.

Awakening unconfuses us.

We're awakened so we can really live before we die.

Those who awake become God's runners, His emissaries, His appointed ambassadors. We've been awakened by His loving voice and fatherly hugs. We're then to be His voice and hugs to others who are still asleep.

Those who awake can fight spiritual battles and win some because we're wary of Satan's tricks and treachery.

Because we're watchful. Because we're prepared for contingencies.

Those who awake can learn to rise above the most distressing circumstances.

Awakened joy is trudging up to the tomb, arms crammed with spices, and finding the huge stone rolled away—and the body gone!

> If God exists, all things are possible, and hope and wonder are appropriate attitudes and not tenderminded illusions.[29]

Final Awakening

We try to stay neutral on this bloody battlefield we call earth. But we're forced into taking sides. Unless we're awakened, we're already playing for the opposing team. We awaken to how we've been duped all these years.

Satan would just as soon we die in our sleep. His objective is to steal whatever suits him, kill whomever gets in his way, and destroy whatever God treasures. And blame God in the process. He lusts for worship. Therefore, the world beyond our own is also a battlefield.[30]

Every thinking person must consider Thomas Hardy's claim that human affairs are too prone to accident, suffering, and disaster for the world to be under the control of a benevolent God. Somerset Maugham voiced the view that he could not believe in a loving God because, he had seen children dying in the hospital diphtheria wards.[31]

But the awakened see life as a favor, not as a given. They see their existence as a gift, not as an accident. They see each day as a wrapped present, not as a right. They see sin as a choice, not as their one shot at happiness.

We all have times when we're snoozing, napping, dozing in and out of reality. We're sawing logs when we should be building the walls of a cathedral. We're counting sheep when we should be following the Shepherd. But awakenings can happen anywhere, any time. And the more we have awakened, the longer we stay awake.

> In the mature personality the pendulum is constantly swinging between wonder and action, and the further it swings in one direction, the further it may go in the opposite direction.[32]

The city of Jerusalem sits on miles of covered sediments. Layer upon layer of whole civilizations lies below each citizen's daily plod. Archeologists and souvenir hunters are ruled by strict laws on how and what and when they can dig, what they must report, and what they can keep. It's a lot of work and trouble, but there's wonder buried down there.

Whether we're digging in the subconscious or studying the story of our lives or the eternal plan, we'll discover multiple layers within and without. Only God knows where the wonder is. He's got to direct our excavations. He'll show us where to put the shovel and begin to dig.

"When anything looks strange, you must look deeper," Falconer would say in *The Musician's Quest*. And no little incident in the narratives of Jesus escaped him. The whole account came alive in his words and thoughts.[33]

If we keep looking under the surface of things, Jesus will help us find under the topsoil the truth that escaped us before. The deeper we dig, the richer the ore. And now and then even the darkest perplexities of our bitter stories can glimmer with a streak of light. And with a lamp at our feet and a light for the path, we keep on track in a trackless world.

Awakening saves a whole lot of time and trouble.

Soon and very soon—the second hand's ticking, the alarm's set, the hour's been chosen—we must fully awake, our assigned tasks completed. To awake means we know what time it is.

We are awakened enough to know we're still outside the real world. Now and then a vision gleams across the soul, but we're on the wrong side of the door. It's like seeing the shadow of a giant hawk passing along the treetops, but when you look up, into the sun, your eyes hurt and you see nothing at all.

> But all the leaves of the New Testament are rustling with the rumour that it will not always be so. Some day, God willing, we shall get *in*.[34]

The last awakening will be the best.

Spirit, open our eyes. Lord, show us the Father and that will be enough for us, "til we cast our crowns before Thee, lost in wonder, love, and praise!"[35]

Exploring the Wonder

1. On a scale of 1 to 10, with 10 being "fully awake" and 1 being "a deadened stupor," how awakened would you judge yourself to be: Mentally? Emotionally? Socially? Spiritually? Discuss this with a close friend who also has read this book. Does he/she agree?

2. What are some of the signs of a spiritually awakened person according to these Scriptures?
    Deuteronomy 7:21
    1 Chronicles 16:9
    Job 42:3
    Psalms 27:4; 42:1–2; 66:5; 68:35; 75:1; 119:120; 150
    Isaiah 29:13–14
    Malachi 2:5–6
    John 15:13
    Galatians 5:22–23
    Philippians 2:4, 9–11
    Hebrews 12:28.

3. What is our part in our own awakenings according to these Scriptures?
    1 Chronicles 16:12–13
    Job 37:14

Psalms 9:1; 119:17–18, 27; 130:1–6
Acts 2:42
Romans 13:11
Ephesians 1:18
Colossians 3:1
2 Corinthians 4:18; 5:16–18
Revelation 3:2

4.   What are some tests of a true spiritual awakening according to these Scriptures? How is the gift of discernment developed, and why is it necessary?
Deuteronomy 13:1–3
Mark 4:13–20
1 Corinthians 14:14–15
Ephesians 6:10–18
1 Thessalonians 2:13
Hebrews 4:12–13
1 Peter 1:22–23
1 John 4:1–3

5.   What are some ways that God aids in the process of awakening?
Psalms 107:8–9; 111:1–9; 136:1–26; 139:5–6
Isaiah 29:23–24; 50:4

6. What are some deterrents to spiritual awakening according to these Scriptures?

Judges 6:3
Psalm 78:11; 42–43
Matthew 21:15
Luke 3:15
2 Corinthians 4:4
2 Thessalonians 1:9–10
Hebrews 2:1–4

7. According to Ezra 3:10–13, why can two different people look at the same thing and one consider it a wonder and the other deem it a disappointment?

8. What are some purposes and benefits of being spiritually awakened according to these Scriptures?

Psalm 78:2–4; 145:4–7
Matthew 13:10–17
John 16:21–22
2 Corinthians 4:16–17
Ephesians 1:9–10, 3:6
1 Thessalonians 5:4–6
Hebrews 10:34
1 Peter 1:6, 2:9
Revelation 2:17, 16:15

9. According to Matthew 17:1–4 and Mark 9:2–8, what is the greatest *spiritual* wonder you ever experienced?

.10. Our bodies require times of rest. Do you think there are times when it's good for our souls or spirits to "sleep"? Explain.

11. Read Luke 1:46–55. This is the response of a spiritually awakened woman. Rewrite her "song" in your own words.

Notes

1. Charles H. Spurgeon, "The Sympathy of the Two Worlds," appendix to *The Glory of Heaven*, by John McArthur (Wheaton, Ill.: Crossway, 1996), 240.
2. Paul Yerden, quoted in "The Worship Gap," by Davis Duggins, *Moody*, March–April 1996, 20.
3. John Sandford and Paula Sandford, *Waking the Slumbering Spirit*, ed. and expanded Norm Bowman (Arlington, Tex.: Clear Stream, 1993), 18.
4. Jean Cocteau, "The Process of Inspiration," in *The Creative Process*, ed. Brewster Ghiselin (Berkeley: Univ. of California Press, 1980), 79.
5. Psalm 45:1.
6. See Genesis 28:17; Exodus 3:6; John 20:26–28; Acts 7:56.

7. Michael Walsh, *Who's Afraid of Classical Music?* (New York: Simon & Schuster, 1989), 36.

8. Louisa May Alcott, quoted in William Anderson, *The World of Louisa May Alcott* (New York: Harper-Perennial, 1992), 31.

9. Brennan Manning, "Cormorants and Kittiwakes," in *The Ragamuffin Gospel* (Sisters, Ore.: Multnomah Books, 1990), 93.

10. John 9:25.

11. Charlie W. Shedd, *Brush of an Angel's Wing* (Ann Arbor, Mich.: Servant, 1994), 183.

12. Frances E. Willard, quoted in *Great Americans in Their Own Words* (New York: Mallard Press, 1990), 228.

13. Charles Colson, *Loving God* (Grand Rapids: Zondervan, 1983), 15.

14. Teresa of Avila, "The River," in *Majestic Is Your Name,* arr. and paraph. David Hazard (Minneapolis: Bethany House, 1993), 156.

15. George MacDonald, *The Baronet's Song,* ed. Michael R. Phillips (Minneapolis: Bethany House, 1983), 21.

16. MacDonald, *The Shepherd's Castle,* ed. Michael R. Phillips (Minneapolis: Bethany House, 1984), 169.

17. Ken Gire, *Windows of the Soul* (Grand Rapids: Zondervan, 1996), 56.

18. Sandford and Sandford, *Waking the Spirit,* 123.

19. Gire, *Windows of the Soul,* 193.

20. Ibid., 49.

21. Harry Blamires, *The Christian Mind* (Ann Arbor, Mich.: Servant, 1963), 41.

22. MacDonald, *The Marquis' Secret,* ed. Michael R. Phillips (Minneapolis: Bethany House, 1982), 58.

23. Sandford and Sandford, *Waking the Slumbering Spirit,* 51.

24. Ibid., 129.

25. Harry Emerson Fosdick, "Making the Best of a Bad Mess," *Twenty Centuries of Great Preaching,* vol. 9 (Waco: Word, 1971), 37.

26. Bradley Baurain, "Nathaniel Hawthorne Probes the Human Heart," *Christianity and the Arts,* August–November 1996, 20.

27. Elizabeth C. Clephane, "Beneath the Cross of Jesus," in *The Hymnal for Worship and Celebration* (Waco: Word, 1986), 183.

28. David Hazard, foreword to *I Promise You a Crown, A Forty-Day Journey with Julian of Norwich* (Minneapolis: Bethany House, 1995), 9.

29. Sam Keen, *Apology for Wonder* (New York: Harper & Row, 1969), 176.

30. See Matthew 4:8–10.

31. Blamires, "The Resurrection," in *On Christian Truth* (Ann Arbor, Mich.: Servant, 1983), 91.

32. Keen, *Apology for Wonder,* 195.

33. MacDonald, *The Musician's Quest* (Minneapolis: Bethany House, 1985), 225.

34. C. S. Lewis, *The Weight of Glory* (New York: Collier, 1980), 17.

35. Charles Wesley, "Love Divine," *The Hymnal for Worship and Celebration* (Waco: Word, 1986), 92.

Note to the Reader